*VISION
AND
REVISION*

# VISION
# AND
# REVISION

Coleridge's Art
of Immanence

*JEAN-PIERRE*
*MILEUR*

UNIVERSITY OF CALIFORNIA PRESS
BERKELEY          LOS ANGELES          LONDON

University of California Press
Berkeley and Los Angeles, California
University of California Press, Ltd.
London, England
© 1982 by
The Regents of the University of California
   Printed in the United States of America

   1   2   3   4   5   6   7   8   9


Library of Congress Cataloging in Publication Data

Mileur, Jean-Pierre.
   Vision and revision.
   Includes bibliographical references and index.
   1. Coleridge, Samuel Taylor, 1772–1834—
Criticism and interpretation.   I. Title.
PR4484.M5        821'.7                81–2487
ISBN 0–520–04447–9                AACR2

# CONTENTS

PREFACE                                                         vii

NOTES ON ABBREVIATIONS                                          xiii

1.  IMAGINATION AND REVISION:
    *Biographia* and the Preface to "Kubla Khan"                 1

2.  "REALITY'S DARK DREAM":
    The Underside of the Conversation Poems                      34

3.  THE PROPHETIC READER AND THE
    PSYCHOLOGICALLY CONTINGENT:
    The Mystery Poems                                            61

4.  BIBLICAL HISTORY AND
    THE AUTHOR'S SHARE:
    *The Statesman's Manual*                                     90

5.  *BIOGRAPHIA LITERARIA* and
    "TO WILLIAM WORDSWORTH":
    Poetry and the Priority of Interpretation                   101

6.  IMAGINATION AS TEXT:
    Poem and Object in *Biographia* XIV                         135

7. THE ORDER OF NATURE AND
THE ORDER OF THE TEXT:
*Biographia* XVII and "Essays on the
Principles of Method"                                    161

8. *CONFESSIONS OF AN INQUIRING
SPIRIT* and *AIDS TO REFLECTION*:
Testament and Testimony                                  174

INDEX                                                    183

# PREFACE

The difficult relationship (to echo Derrida) between the Being Writing and the Written Being becomes most problematical for us as students of Coleridge when he insists on confessing to misdemeanors of which, on the basis of our responses to the texts, he is innocent. As in the preface to "Kubla Khan," Coleridge seems determined to block our efforts to give him the credit he deserves. Even when he does not contradict us directly, his willingness to sustain inconsistency, even contradiction, within a loose or fragmentary form and his tendency to write himself into and out of other men's texts make it difficult to articulate our sense of Coleridge's value in terms other than those provided by the texts themselves, as difficult and problematical as they are.

This essay is not intended to be exhaustive either in its treatment of available primary sources or in its employment of the tremendous volume of criticism, much of it very good, that has grown up around Coleridge's writings. Rather it sets for itself the narrower task of tracing through a variety of works from the early, middle, and late careers the development of that implicit or immanent Coleridge who comes into being and lives out his fate in the dialogue of text with text. Ultimately, this immanence is represented less as a personality, in terms of psychological categories and conflicts, than as a problematic—a field within which certain "intellectual" problems are privileged with an emotional intensity of the kind normally associated with purely personal, internal con-

*viii* flict. The familiar Coleridgean concerns—with imagination, with representation, with religion and philosophy—become most problematical and most interesting to Coleridge where they approach the Protean problem of immanence: immanence of the author in his work, of identity in consciousness, of God in his creation. Of course, immanence is not comprehended in any act of representation, as I may have seemed to imply two sentences back; rather, immanence stands in surety for representation itself. It is immanence that gives the text its distinctiveness, bestowing a human-seeming inwardness and the attributes of intentionality on an object that actually has neither psyche nor will.

Our immediate purpose then must be to identify that tendentiousness that (initially, at least) is less an attribute of Coleridge's understanding of his work than of the dialogue between texts. The eclectic method that this pursuit demands reveals an increasing willingness on Coleridge's part to accept the implications and to become a student of his own immanence. In chapters 2 and 3, we will discuss the Mystery Poems as devastating critiques of Coleridge's own poetic practice in the Conversation Poems. Unable to deny responsibility for the poems and unable to accept their implications about his limitations as an artist and the rootlessness of imagination in the natural world, Coleridge becomes increasingly alienated from his own poetry. In the period often associated with his greatest productivity, the suppression of "Christabel" and "Kubla Khan" and his willingness to accept overly harsh verdicts on "The Rime of the Ancient Mariner" indicate the degree to which Coleridge's immanence shocks and contradicts the desires of the man. Yet whether it appears as benign or demonic, this immanence also displays a consistency of concern and creative purpose that all too often eludes Coleridge when the burdened man attempts to explain to his public what he has done or is going to do in his writings.

Coleridge eventually comes to see that the often disturbing distinction, even contradiction, between his identity and his immanence is not a sign of his own defective creative will but a consequence of man's position in the world. This book begins with (and elaborates upon, in chapters 5 to 7) the text and event that mark this change in attitude most clearly: *Biographia Literaria* and the intense period of renewed creativity of 1815–17. Initially, our main concern is with the much-discussed belatedness of the secondary imagination—taken by some commentators as a sign of Coleridge's own sense of crushing inadequacy in the face of Wordsworth's poetic superiority. But this belatedness ceases to be an embarrassment when considered not in relation to the visionary ambitions of Milton or Wordsworth but to the ceaseless creative confirmation of God's identity, I AM. In this context, the self-confirmation of the Wordsworthian poetic and the absence of such confirmation in Coleridge's own work are equally insignificant. Revision—important to Coleridge as a concept and as an activity at this time—is the positive face that he puts on the belatedness of the individual will in relation to simple being, in relation to history, and ultimately, in relation to God's sustaining creativity. Revision indicates the acceptance and active exploitation of a secondariness inherent in our condition.

The result is a document of which Wordsworth would simply have been incapable. Coleridge succeeds in all but eliminating the "auto-" element from *Biographia Literaria*, determining that what he has read is as important as what he has written (indeed, is sometimes identical with it), or whom he married, or when he was born. Things are selected out of the totality of his experience (including imaginative experience) without reference to a hierarchy determined by a greater or lesser degree of pertinence to the individual man, Samuel Taylor Coleridge. Self-representation is reconceived at a distance from personal history and psychology, in terms of the mutual immanence of culture and self. Culture and self more than mirror each other in *Biographia*: Coleridge bestows on the culture he knows his own uniquely human pathos and receives in return culture's incredibly various power to be manifest.

In Coleridge's mature understanding of the text, not even his own words are privileged simply because they are his, and, more to the point, not even his own presence in the text is privileged simply because he is its author. Thus, Coleridge is finally able to face up to and exorcise Wordsworth from his writings, concluding that Wordsworth is the greater poet because he is the blinder man. Less blinded by the need to assert his distinctive poetic identity, Coleridge is the greater reader—as prophetic a reader as Wordsworth is a poet. The immanence of Wordsworth in Coleridge's work, representing his own egotistical demands on writing and cul-

x  ture, is no longer allowed to stand between him and a recognition
of the power to be derived from conceiving the self in terms of
immanence, rather than distinct (and defensive) identity.

At the end of *The Prelude*, Wordsworth envisions the fulfillment of his destiny as poet-prophet as a talking down to the multitude below. He becomes the prophet of nature as an elevating alternative to the confusions of social life and the disappointments of
history. Coleridge, on the other hand, sees himself as more prophetic
as he immerses (perhaps disperses) himself even more deeply into
his culture and its history. For Coleridge, the prophetic reader's
willingness to find himself in the pathos immanent in the text and
to offer himself as the vehicle of its fulfillment reflects the biblical prophet's gift not for self-enhancing historical prediction or
spiritual leadership but for experiencing his own life and the history of his times in terms of God's pathos. The prophetic reader answers the text's search for fulfillment in the same way that the
man for whom to understand is to believe confirms the historical
identity of the Bible.

Chapters 4, 7, and 8 deal specifically with the role of the
Bible in bringing about the transformations in attitude that we
have been discussing. For Coleridge, the immanence or Written
Being is governed by the ontology not of language per se but of
the special category, text, which is privileged for civilized men because it is the vehicle for the continued immanence of the Bible in
all aspects of our experience as historical and cultural beings. This
special relationship is based on the historical origin of what we call
the text in God's revelation of his own immanence. The original,
biblical text is the means by which God inserts himself into earthly
temporality (thus creating history). In the context of the Bible, history thus becomes the closest thing to a psychology of God that human beings are capable of imagining—an account of his immanence.

In the final chapter, we conclude by discussing those late
works—*Aids to Reflection* and *Confessions of an Inquiring Spirit*—
in which the question of the nature of the Bible subsumes the
earlier psychological, poetic, and philosophical formulations of the
problematic of immanence, which had proved, each in its own in-
structive way, to be inadequate. Approaching what he takes to be
the ultimate implications of the problems faced in his own career,
Coleridge is able to redeem from the conflict between immanence

and identity many of the motifs signifying his self-division in earlier, more burdened works. In doing this, he is at last able to achieve a marriage of sorts between a philosophical, historical, and theological understanding of the Bible and the existential plight of the desiring and limited individual.

I would like to take this opportunity to thank John Guillory, Harold Bloom, Ronald Paulson, and Leslie Brisman, who read and made valuable comments on this essay in its original form; my colleagues Edwin Eigner, Robert Essick, Laura Brown, and John Ganim, who contributed substantially to subsequent revisions; and the Committee on Research of the University of California, Riverside, which provided funding for the preparation of the manuscript.

# NOTE ON ABBREVIATIONS

For convenience, the following abbreviations will be used when referring to frequently cited works by Coleridge:

BL    *Biographia Literaria*, ed. John T. Shawcross, 2 vols. (Oxford: Oxford University Press, 1907).

CIS   *Confessions of an Inquiring Spirit*, ed. H. St. J. Hart (Stanford: Stanford University Press, 1967).

EPM   "Essays on the Principles of Method," vol. 1 of *The Friend*, in *The Collected Works of Samuel Taylor Coleridge*, vol. 4, ed. Barbara E. Rooke (Princeton: Princeton University Press, 1969).

SM    *The Statesman's Manual*, in *The Collected Works of Samuel Taylor Coleridge*, vol. 6, ed. R. J. White (Princeton: Princeton University Press, 1972).

For all references to the texts of the poems, see *The Complete Poetical Works of Samuel Taylor Coleridge*, vol. 1, ed. E. H. Coleridge (Oxford: Oxford University Press, 1912).

# I

## IMAGINATION AND REVISION:

### Biographia and the Preface to "Kubla Khan"

In 1816, "Kubla Khan" and "Christabel" appeared in print for the first time. Just over a year later *Biographia Literaria*, Coleridge's answer to Wordsworth's *Prelude*, appeared along with *Sibylline Leaves*, which included the new gloss to "The Rime of the Ancient Mariner." Thus, 1817 marked the first year in which Coleridge had committed to print the major poems of the canon in substantially the form in which we know them today.

In the introduction to his edition of *Biographia Literaria*, George Watson argues that "Coleridge seems from the beginning to have regarded the *Biographia* as a whole, if not as a preface in the conventional sense, at least as a companion volume to his collection of verse."[1] In support of this contention, Watson points to a letter written by Coleridge to Byron in 1815: "A general preface will be prefixed (to the volume of verse), on the principles of philosophic and general criticism relatively to the fine arts in general; but especially to poetry...."[2] That this refers to the intended relationship between *Biographia* and *Sibylline Leaves* is further suggested by the fact that

---

[1] Samuel Taylor Coleridge, *Biographia Literaria*, ed. George Watson (New York: Dutton, 1971), p. xiv.

[2] Watson, ed., *Biographia Literaria*, p. xiv, n. The complete letter, dated October 17, 1815, can be found in *The Unpublished Letters of Samuel Taylor Coleridge*, ed. Earle Leslie Griggs (New Haven: Yale University Press, 1933), II, 142–46.

2

the sheets for *Sibylline Leaves*, printed for Gutch by John Evans of Bristol in 1815, appeared two years later with the then meaningless register "Vol. ii" in their signatures. Apparently this volume was meant to follow upon a one-volume *Biographia*, the two to represent the author's literary achievement—a splendid reply to the repeated and deeply-resented charges of idleness.[3]

Coleridge clearly regarded the combination of *Biographia* and *Sibylline Leaves* as a summary statement on his twenty years as a poet and philosopher. And in the period 1815–17, when *Biographia* was being written and both volumes prepared for the press, he was engaged in the task of interpreting and giving shape to his own career.

One of the book's central concerns is the integration of Coleridge's efforts as poet and philosopher. In Volume I he shows how his early poetic interests led him deeper into the philosophy of the mind. His refutation of Hartley and associational psychology leads us by way of Kant and Schelling to his famous distinctions between imagination and fancy and between primary and secondary imagination. In Volume II his theory of the imagination provides one of the bases for his critique of Wordsworth and leads to the concept of the organic form of the poem. Presumably, the publication of *Biographia* and *Sibylline Leaves* as a two-volume set was to demonstrate a similar integration of poetry and philosophy: in the "sibylline leaves" of the poems, we read the prophetic fragments of the realized poet-philosopher of *Biographia* while the context provided by *Biographia* presents an interpretation of Coleridge and his concerns by which the poems are to be read anew. The conclusion that we are to draw from this is that Coleridge is not so much abandoning poetry as he is pursuing the implications of his poetic practice beyond the bounds of the conventionally poetic.

In his attempt to throw a controlling net of meaning around his career and its fragmented results, Coleridge is engaged at an amazingly comprehensive level in a revision-by-context of his

[3] Watson, ed., *Biographia Literaria*, p. xiv.

self-image and of all his work to that time. Through his prose Coleridge seeks to provide a new context in which his poems are to be read—a context constituting a *revision* of the poems in the most literal sense of the word: a seeing again, enlisting them in the service of a newer, more comprehensive vision of his own identity as poet-philosopher.

At the center of Volume I of *Biographia Literaria* is Coleridge's refutation of Hartley and his associational psychology. Although he is willing to admit that "in our perceptions we seem to ourselves merely passive to an external power, whether as a mirror reflecting the landscape or a blank canvas on which some unknown hand paints it" (*BL*, I, 66), Coleridge questions the sufficiency of a model based on this fact. If we accept the idea that the mind is entirely composed of impressions received through the senses and that the association of ideas within the mind is determined by the fact that certain impressions are linked together by having been perceived at the same time, then "our whole life would be divided between the despotism of outward impressions and that of senseless and passive memory" (*BL*, I, 77).

Coleridge's ultimate concern in his refutation of Hartley is with the freedom of the will. If we assume that the will and all acts of thought and intention "are parts and products of this blind mechanism, instead of being distinct powers whose function is to control, determine and modify the phantasmal chaos of association," then the soul is "present only to be pinched and stroked, while the very squeals or purring are produced by an agency wholly independent and alien" (*BL*, I, 81). Coleridge extends the associationist conception to include the idea of a will which "by confining and intensifying the attention may arbitrarily give vividness or distinctness to any object whatsoever." Therefore:

> The true practical law of association is this, that whatever makes certain parts of a total impression more vivid or distinct than the rest will determine the mind to recall these in preference to others equally linked together by the common condition of contemporaneity or (what I deem a more appropriate and philosophical term) continuity. (*BL*, I, 87)

4    Out of Coleridge's passive perception and active will grows this early formulation of the imagination as the faculty that partakes both of the active and the passive and that is the agency by which the focus of mental activity moves from one to the other:

> Most of my readers will have observed a small water-insect on the surface of rivulets which throws a cinque-spotted shadow fringed with prismatic colors on the sunny bottom of the brook; and will have noticed how the little animal wins its way up against the stream, by alternate pulses of active and passive motion, now resisting the current, and now yielding to it in order to gather strength and a momentary fulcrum for a further propulsion. This is no unapt emblem for the mind's self-experience in the act of thinking. There are evidently two powers at work which relatively to each other are active and passive. (In philosophical language we must denominate this intermediate faculty in all its degrees and determinations the imagination. But in common language, and especially on the subject of poetry, we appropriate the name to a superior degree of the faculty, joined to a superior voluntary control over it. (*BL*, I, 85–86)

The final lines of this passage look quite definitely forward to the much more famous formulation of imagination in Chapter XIII. Also of considerable importance, as we will see shortly, is Coleridge's reference to "the mind's self-experience," suggesting a certain awareness of self as an experience or pattern detachable from its own essence.

But the immediate consequence of Coleridge's distinction between perception and will is his confrontation with the problem of dualism. Coleridge seems to object less to dualism itself than to the implications of a materialism that draws an absolute distinction between mind and matter. If we are to accept such a radical distinction, it becomes very difficult indeed to show how "any affection from without can metamorphoze itself into perception or will" (*BL*, 1, 90). Without some common ground between them, it is impossible to explain the power of external impressions over the will or the power of the will over perception. In order to do so in 5 such a system, we must either mistake "distinct images for clear conceptions" (*BL*, I, 91) or deprive matter of its character in an attempt to identify it with thought. Instead Coleridge suggests that body and spirit are "no longer absolutely heterogeneous but may, without any absurdity, be supposed to be different modes or degrees in perfection of a common substratum" (*BL*, I, 91). Coleridge is not only looking back to his earlier formulation of imagination as the mediating factor between active and passive states of mind, partaking of both, but forward to his division of the imagination itself into primary and secondary.

Through Chapter XII and into the first part of Chapter XIII, Coleridge's main concern is still the reconciliation of "I am" with "it is," which, as Thomas McFarland has observed, is the central endeavor of Coleridge's philosophy.[4] Then this argument is broken off, and we confront that curious letter from "a friend whose practical judgment I have ample reason to estimate and revere" (*BL*, I, 198), who is, of course, Coleridge himself. This interruption also serves as a preface to Coleridge's celebrated definitions of imagination and fancy:

The IMAGINATION then, I consider either as primary, or secondary. The primary IMAGINATION I hold to be the living Power and prime Agent of all human Perception, and as a repetition in the finite mind of the eternal act of creation in the infinite I AM. The secondary Imagination I consider as an echo of the former, co-existing with the conscious will, yet still as identical with the primary in the *kind* of its agency, and differing only in *degree*, and in the *mode* of its operation. It dissolves, diffuses, dissipates, in order to re-create; or where this process is rendered impossible, yet still at all events it struggles to idealize and unify. It is essentially *vital*, even as all objects (*as* objects) are essentially fixed and dead.

---

[4] Thomas McFarland, "The Origin and Significance of Coleridge's Theory of the Secondary Imagination," in *New Perspectives on Coleridge and Wordsworth: Selected Essays from the English Institute*, ed. Geoffrey H. Hartman (New York: Columbia University Press, 1972), p. 198.

6    FANCY, on the contrary, has no other counters to play with, but fixities and definites. The Fancy is indeed no other than a mode of Memory emancipated from the order of time and space; while it is blended with, and modified by that empirical phenomenon of the will, which we express by the word CHOICE. But equally with the ordinary memory the Fancy must receive all its materials ready made from the law of association.  (*BL*, I, 202)

As the "primary agent of all human perception," the primary imagination is presumably the imagination's link with the outside world, making images and impressions available to the secondary imagination. But the primary imagination is not merely a passive receiver of images from the senses; it is generative in a way that is compared with a godlike expression of self in a continuous act of creation. And just as each of God's creations is a confirmation of his identity, the images and thoughts generated by the primary imagination are evidences or confirmations of the self's concrete existence—of the literality of consciousness. In short, the primary imagination is an internalization of "it is." After all, "I am" is only the self's recognition that it too has an existence as an "it is." Therefore, the primary imagination can be seen as that element of imagination that possesses images and perceptions in order to regenerate them as its own products so that they may be seen as confirmations of the mind's sense of its own existence.

The expression in the "finite mind" of the "eternal act of creation in the infinite I AM" not only attributes a ceaseless creative richness to the primary imagination but also argues that this richness is the finite fragment intimating the generative richness of God's higher order. The implication is that the inner structure of the self is the basis in each man's self-experience potentially providing the basis for belief in and perception of a higher unity.

At first glance, there is a bewildering confusion in Coleridge's statements about the secondary imagination. He calls it an echo of the primary imagination, differing only in degree. Yet its capacity to dissolve, dissipate, and recreate—to idealize and unify —argues otherwise. Presumably, it is the material provided by the primary imagination that is being dissolved and recreated, so

Coleridge's insistence that the secondary imagination is an echo of the primary must have a rather idiosyncratic meaning.

The "echo" of the secondary imagination is clearly an attempt to distinguish a more subtle concept of "repetition." To this end, Coleridge coined in *The Statesman's Manual* (significantly enough, in connection with his definition of "symbol") the term "tautegorical," meaning to repeat with a difference (*SM,* 30n). Echoing, extending, and transforming, the secondary imagination is fundamentally revisionary in nature. The relationship between something and its revision is unmistakable, as is the final distinction between the two; and it is this relationship that Coleridge seeks to name with his neologism. Thus, the primary metaphor for the relationship between primary and secondary imagination is that of the original and its revision.

Some*thing* is a key word here because revision can only be performed on a thing, an "it is," a text already existing as an object. The primary imagination makes perceptions available to the secondary imagination as things susceptible of reflection. This requires a certain dualism in the mind—a distance allowing the mind to contemplate its own contents as part of an objectified self that is experientially distinct from the controlling, artificing will. If the primary imagination is somehow prior to the operation of the conscious will, it is also of the self and not of the external world. Distinguishing self from the conscious will, primary imagination thus becomes a principle of self-abnegation, a suspension of will, guaranteeing consciousness of its own literality. The addition of the secondary imagination issues in a Coleridgean *Cogito,* in which it is not thinking but thinking insofar as it is a form of revision, which is the guaranty of identity.

Because fancy receives its materials "ready made from the law of association," it involves no objectification and no revision—no control of self over the world. Fancy represents mind at the mercy of image as direct experience. It is this quality of being possessed by the immalleable and self-sufficient materials of perception to which Coleridge refers when he says that fancy has no other counters "to play with, but fixities and definites": this is not an inherent attribute of the counters but of the faculty that lacks the power to transform impressions and thus becomes their prisoner.

8     As a "mode of memory emancipated from the order of time and space," fancy is nonetheless limited by the already-perceived in the same sense that memory is limited by the already-experienced. Its "emancipation" bespeaks the disorientation resulting when consciousness is conceived as pure function—in this case, the capacity to choose among associations—unaccommodated to any sense of a locus or space proper to consciousness.

Fancy's positive contribution to our understanding of imagination is related to the question of choice. Coleridge's distinction between primary and secondary imagination does not imply a *choice* between them. It is only when fancy enters the picture as an equally internalized and fundamental possibility of *not* being imaginative that the possibility of normative choice arises, and the locus of value is identified within the self. Furthermore, fancy is intimately linked with the secondary imagination by the fact that just as it is displaced from the privileged space of imagination, secondary imagination is permanently displaced from an original act of creation/perception in the primary imagination. Thus, fancy and secondary imagination share a belatedness, redeemed in the case of the latter by the power of revision.

Virtually everything normally comprehended in the concept of consciousness falls within the limits of secondary imagination or its contrary, fancy. It is the peculiar nature of the primary imagination to define the space in which world is transformed into consciousness. The primary imagination is at once the origin of consciousness and by definition inaccessible—after all, any attempt to apprehend it is *already* well within the realm of consciousness. Thus it is the fate of the secondary imagination to exist perpetually in the already-begun and to posit out of its own sense of belatedness its necessary pretext, the primary imagination. Nevertheless, the awareness of its own belatedness inherent in Coleridge's concept of imagination redeems the will from the trivial arbitrariness at the heart of mere fancy.

Coleridge's anti-Cartesian *Cogito* evades a direct opposition of mind and material through internalization. In a characteristic Romantic maneuver, Coleridge subsumes opposition into an analogy of oppositions, re-creating the possibility of a hierarchy of analogues linking the innermost order of the self with a cosmic order. Central to such a hierarchy is the analogy, clearly intended in the notion of primary imagination, between human and divine creativity. In order to make this analogy, Coleridge's definition glosses over its own most important observation: for all its richness, the primary imagination is nonetheless finite by comparison with God's eternal creation. The inaccessibility of the infinite to the finite is echoed then in the inaccessibility of the primary imagination—the place where human and divine creation are revealed to be analogous—to consciousness. What Coleridge's definition of imagination does then is to name as its own peculiar place this break in the chain of being, this fundamental discontinuity determining the belated, revisionary nature of consciousness. The inability of consciousness to conceive adequately its own origin or pretext in terms of original creation is reflected in the fact that primary imagination is also largely revisionary in its relation to sense impression.

Coleridge's definition of imagination is properly (and literally) central to *Biographia Literaria* because it internalizes at a level prior to consciousness itself a revisionary relationship between text, pretext, and context that is everywhere apparent in the undertakings of 1815–18. Indeed, my choice of "revision" instead of the more conventionally philosophical "reflection" is intended to convey the conviction that Coleridge's conception of the space proper to consciousness, of the nature of the discontinuity in the chain of being, and, as we will see, in the continuity of human history, is textual in nature. This largely accounts for the intimacy and occasional interchangeability of Coleridge's concerns with the philosophy of the mind, with his own past literary production, with the nature of the language employed within the space defined by the concept of the text, and, eventually, with the nature of the Bible as a text.

I have already discussed the way in which *Biographia* becomes the revisionary context of the poems of *Sibylline Leaves*. In light of our discussion of imagination, it would seem that the failure of the two books to come together neatly into the projected two-volume metatext reflects the degree to which the problematics of revision are confounded with the gap between an act of creation and the confirmation of identity in that creation. As we will see

*10*    in the following chapters, the relationship between the Mystery Poems and the rest of the canon also takes the form of a revisionary interpretation of Coleridge's own poetic practice. It is also likely that even as *Sibylline Leaves* was being prepared for press and *Biographia* being written, Coleridge was adding the gloss to "The Rime of the Ancient Mariner" and the preface to "Kubla Khan"—two more instances of contextual revision. Even closer to home, there is in the letter prefacing the discussion of imagination still another instance of this reluctance to let the text speak for itself—still another instance of the confrontation between Coleridge and his text spinning out of itself revisionary pretexts and contexts, grasping at an ever-elusive immanence.

    *Biographia* XIII begins with an epigraph, taken from Raphael's speech on the one light in *Paradise Lost* V:

> O Adam, One Almighty is, from whom
> All things proceed and up to him return,
> If not depraved from good: created all
> Such to perfection, one first nature all,
> Indued with various forms, various degrees
> Of substance, and, in things that live, of life;
> But more refin'd, more spirituous and pure,
> As nearer to him plac'd, or nearer tending,
> Each in their several active spheres assign'd,
> Till body up to spirit work, in bounds
> Proportion'd to each kind. So from the root
> Springs lighter the green stalk, from thence the leaves
> More airy: last the bright consummate flower
> Spirit odorous breathes. Flowers and their fruit,
> Man's nourishment, by gradual scale sublim'd,
> To *vital* spirits aspire: to *animal*:
> To *intellectual*!—give both life and sense,
> Fancy and understanding; whence the soul
> Reason receives, and reason is her *being*,
> Discursive or intuitive.

(*BL*, I, 195)

These lines emphasize the hierarchical order of God's creation—a creation organized into a hierarchy by a unity that is at once its root, its pinnacle, its substance, and its context. But the organic analogy at the speech's center owes more to Dante than to botany, for the very presence of the angelic messenger marks the point at which the organicism of the hierarchy breaks down. Adam's reason does not allow him to evolve this insight for himself; it only allows him to recognize the truth of revelation when it comes—to recognize for what it is a message from across the gulf separating God and Man. Raphael's presence in the epigraph mocks in advance the Descartes who "speaking as a naturalist, and in imitation of Archimedes, says, give me matter and motion and I will construct you the universe" (*BL*, I, 195–96). Moreover, it suggests that there is not as much distance as might be supposed between the hubris of Descartes and the transcendental philosopher who says: "grant me a nature having two contrary forces, the one of which tends to expand infinitely, while the other strives to apprehend or find itself in this infinity, and I will cause the world of intelligences with the whole system of their representations to rise up before you" (*BL*, I, 196). The intimated discontinuity between ratiocination and revelation suggests from the very beginning the futility of Coleridge's own attempt to derive intelligence and its "system of . . . representations" from within.

It is certainly true of the beginning of *Biographia* XIII that no one ever wished it longer. Indeed, it seems to go on just long enough to demonstrate its own futility. In this context, the problem of *Biographia* XIII becomes not so much to derive intelligence but to extend it to comprehend its own limitations in relation to revelation. It can certainly be argued that the relationship between primary and secondary imagination seeks to internalize the relationship between reason tied to consciousness and revelation tied to something preconscious, linking self to other.

Only three pages or so go by before Coleridge's transcendentalizing is interrupted by the letter from a friend. Leslie Brisman has said of the letter's effect:

Reaching beyond overdetermined, Schellingesque prose, Coleridge finds a new, mediate verbal space. Michel Foucault writes that "between the already encoded eye and reflexive knowledge there is a middle region which liberates order itself." Like Foucault's "middle region," Coleridge's middle voice defines a new freedom—and a new anteriority, restoring in those definitions of imagination and fancy what Foucault calls something "more solid, more archaic, less dubious, always more true than the theories that attempt to give those expressions explicit form, exhaustive application, or philosophical foundation." Coleridge's definitions emerge out of and beyond the rhetoric of exhaustive philosophical foundation, and though they borrow from German sources, restore us to a point of origin before philosophic rhetoric.[5]

On the basis of this argument, it would seem that if the personalizing of the chapter's rhetoric in the letter does not remove German ideas, it at least provides a context in which those ideas can be liberated from the limitations of philosophical rhetoric. But Brisman argues that:

if the disquisition before the break in the *Biographia* chapter is to a dangerous extent paraphrasing Schelling, then it is only in the "friend's" letter that Coleridge seems to speak in his own (more child-like and friendly) voice.[6]

Brisman goes on to say that the relaxation of intellectual will that allows this more "natural" Coleridge to take over "is to some extent a fall. The voice of practical judgment is a lesser voice, a sensible Understanding in distinction from a higher Reason."[7]

This is, I think, not quite accurate (though it points up the problem admirably). Coleridge's letter does not substitute itself for the operation of the higher reason; it substitutes for the flow of philosophical rhetoric the point of realization (still 100 pages

---

[5] Leslie Brisman, *Romantic Origins* (Ithaca: Cornell University Press, 1978), p. 36.

[6] Ibid., p. 34.

[7] Ibid., pp. 34–35.

away if we continue to proceed in the same manner) that restores the rift between Coleridge the philosopher and Coleridge the man. The letter, like the gloss to "The Rime of the Ancient Mariner" and the preface to "Kubla Khan," bespeaks a self-alienation, a failure to recognize himself in what he is writing or has written. In at least one of its functions, the attribution of the letter to a friend reflects the degree of Coleridge's self-alienation.

Displaced onto the fictitious friend, the letter returns us to a problem prior to that of reconciling contraries into a *tertium aliquid*: the presence in the text of Raphael, or of Schelling, or of another Coleridge—of some other agency—at the point of realization. The letter places Coleridge in a relation to his friend much like that of Raphael to Adam. This is less a form of self-promotion than an indication of the problems involved in being both the agent and recipient of revelation, both writer and reader, as any author must be.

Coleridge's friend begins by describing the effects of his perusal of the original chapter (of 100 pages). Admitting that he did not understand it, the friend goes on to describe the extreme degree of intellectual disorientation caused by Coleridge's unusual opinions and method of argument. But the most interesting and striking part of the letter involves the friend's feelings, which, he says:

> I cannot better represent than by supposing myself to have known only our light airy modern chapels of ease, and then for the first time to have been placed, and left alone, in one of our largest gothic cathedrals in a gusty moonlight night of autumn. "Now in glimmer, and now in gloom"; often in palpable darkness not without a chilly sensation of terror; then suddenly emerging into broad yet visionary lights with colored shadows, of fantastic shapes, yet all decked with holy insignia and mystic symbols; and ever and anon coming out full upon pictures and stone-work images of great men, with whose names I was familiar but which looked upon me with countenances and an expression, the most dissimilar to all I had been in the habit of connecting to those names. Those whom I had been taught to venerate as almost super-human in magni-

tude of intellect I found perched in little fret-work niches, as grotesque dwarfs; while the grotesques, in my hither-to belief, stood guarding the high altar with all the characters of Apotheosis. In short, what I had supposed substances were thinned away into shadows, while everywhere shadows were deepened into substances:

If substance may be called that shadow seem'd,
For each seemed either!

*Milton*

Yet after all, I could not but repeat the lines which you had quoted from a MS. poem of your own in *The Friend* and applied to a work of Mr. Wordsworth's, though with a few of the words altered:
————An orphic tale indeed,
A tale obscure of high and passionate thoughts
To a strange music chanted!

(*BL*, I, 199–200)

In all of Coleridge's works only the preface to "Kubla Khan" represents such a sustained attempt to redefine the grounds of an experience by creating a sense of the alien and strange. This image of familiar figures placed in the new context of the gothic cathedral suggests the letter's role as the new, transforming context of the remarks on imagination that follow. This half of the letter strives to create by its strangeness a sense of the magnitude of the change wrought in perception even by the uncomprehending reading of the entire manuscript chapter. The interplay of shadow and substance toward the end of this passage serves as an emblem for the way in which it transforms the subsequent remarks on imagination: it turns the present substance into the shadow of a much greater magnitude. This method of supplying a new context which transforms what is present into a symbol for what is greater but fundamentally inaccessible—the present fragment into an embodiment of a whole which, by its very nature, is lost as soon as it is experienced—is a method adopted by Coleridge in his revisions of "Kubla Khan" and "The Rime of the Ancient Mariner."

I have already had occasion to make reference to Keats's phrase "the shadow of a magnitude" from his poem on the Elgin Marbles.[8] In this poem, the fragmented remains of Greek civilization are identified with the poet's own small, fragmented output. Looking back at all that is embodied in those few marble fragments, the poet sees in his own poetic fragments a similar promise of a future whole. Such a way of making the seen stand for the unseen is central to Coleridge's philosophical method. Interested in combining a basically mystical world view with a rational method,[9] he was obviously in need of a means of using the comprehensible fragment to represent the apparently incomprehensible whole. The importance of this perception in Coleridge's view of his own method is reflected in the following passage from the fourth of his "Essays on the Principles of Method":

> [He is describing the ways in which a great mind can be recognized.] It is the unpremeditated and evidently habitual arrangement of his words, grounded on the habit of foreseeing, in each integral part, or (more plainly) in every sentence, the whole that he then intends to communicate. However irregular and desultory his talk, there is method in his fragments. (EPM, 449)

Each fragmentary part is arranged to intimate the eventual whole. But Coleridge's interest in this method, at least as far as his theological concerns go, is in the power of present fragments to intimate a whole which, by its very nature, is not available. It is not difficult to see in such remarks a suggestion of Coleridge's idea of organic form. But the route we have taken to reach this point indicates that at least in one sense, organic form means something entirely different to Coleridge from what we commonly understand it to mean.

If existence conforms to an organic and not a mechanical

---

8 John Keats, "On Seeing the Elgin Marbles" (1817), line 14.
9 McFarland, "Origin and Significance of Coleridge's Theory," pp. 199–204.

*16*    model, then the leaf is the fragment from which the tree can be reconstructed (hence, *Sibylline Leaves*), and access to a higher truth can be obtained through what is present and available to the senses and understanding. At the root of Coleridge's idea of organic form is the paradox that although human consciousness is basically fragmented, imagination working through the understanding and the senses can intimate a higher unity beyond.

This brings us back to Coleridge's interest in the reconciliation of "I Am" and "it is." An absolute distinction between inner and outer life would deny the ability of those present fragments to intimate an absent whole. But if the ultimate unity of existence could be visualized as a series of linked and dynamic opposites (though not contradictories), then each opposition could be seen to imply the other and so on, until a picture of that ultimate unity began to emerge. The first step, taken in his definitions of imagination and fancy, is to define such an opposition within the self.

It is from within the heart of this definition, from within the gap separating finite from infinite, that the ideological importance of the fragment emerges. That gap between the pinnacle of the comprehensible chain of being and God himself makes of any human order a fragment. Whether we are tracing in God's visible creation the great hierarchy of being, or attempting to construct, à la Descartes, a cosmology out of a few basic facts, ratiocination must at some point give way to revelation, the evidence of things seen to the evidence of the unseen.

In this context, the structure of God's order and the method for reconstructing it had to be reconceived. The continuous and systematic combining of smaller or limited phenomena into larger phenomena had to be replaced by a conception linking God and man not through the visible world but through the invisible preconditions of comprehensibility. If we turn back for a moment to Coleridge's remarks on the conversation of genius, it becomes apparent that Coleridge treats the fragments of a discourse as prophecies of the ultimate import of the whole. What Coleridge's method demands then is the interpretation of the prophetic fragments of an immanence and not the articulation of a hierarchy, all of whose parts are simultaneously and already manifest in our experience of the world and of ourselves.

The "table," to use Foucault's term,[10] upon which such interpretation is possible, upon which Coleridge's method is operable, is defined by the nature of the text as something distinct from world, self, and even language per se. As I will endeavor to show in a later chapter, the context in which imagination emerges as a fundamental Coleridgean concept is not finally the self's experience of itself but the self's experience of texts that are undeniably of it without being one with it. Once it is understood that in the key period of Coleridge's career, textuality is emerging as a fundamental category of apprehension, the greater significance of his pun on "leaves" becomes apparent. The sibylline leaves are not the leaves of a tree but the pages of a book. If the tree may be inferred from the leaf, it is a good deal less certain that the book can be derived from the page, the corpus from a single poem, or the nature of the author from his text. Thus the text itself, which provides the context within which imagination and method come into being, is the anomaly in the order for which Coleridge strives.

Thus Coleridge offers his definition of imagination not in an "autobiographia literaria" but at the halfway point in a "biographia literaria"—a book exploring the relationship between the coming into being of an author and the coming into being of a book, in a world already crowded with authors and books. Among these authors, the foremost is Wordsworth, who had built up an impressive corpus by 1817. It is, I think, important to recognize in Coleridge's "letter from a friend" a reference to an important Wordsworthian text, the preface to the 1814 edition of *The Excursion*:

> the two works (*Prelude* and *Recluse*) have the same kind of relation to each other, if he may so express himself, as the ante-chapel has to the body of a gothic church. Continuing this allusion, he may be permitted to add, that his minor pieces, which have been long before the Public, when they shall be properly arranged, will be found by the attentive reader to have such connection with the main work, as may give them claim to be likened to the little

[10] Michel Foucault, *The Order of Things*, trans. anon. (New York: Random House, 1973), p. xvii.

18 cells, oratories, and sepulchral recesses, ordinarily included in those edifices.[11]

Just as *The Prelude* envisioned the resolution of life into vocation, bringing us to the threshold of the self-allegorization comprehended in the notion of career, Wordsworth's Preface envisions the resolution of individual poems written at different times into the simultaneous whole implicit in the architectural metaphor. Wordsworth's culmination transcends the identities of individual texts, subordinating text to figuration, and figuration to his own will to self-allegorization.

The most immediate difference between Coleridge's use of the gothic cathedral figure and Wordsworth's is basically one of viewpoint. Whereas Wordsworth confidently asserts the possibility of viewing his own career from without, from the vantage point provided by a culminating figure, Coleridge locates himself inside the figure, serving notice that we are permanently in the realm of mediation. This shift in perspective suggests that figuration is not an instrument we use so much as the substance of our condition. Coleridge intimates that once we begin subordinating texts to figures or lives to allegories of career, we are eventually brought to wonder what the self is an image of.

But the gap between Coleridge, the author of definitions of the imagination, and Coleridge, the disoriented "friend," also intimates that the ease of Wordsworth's self-recognition is equally unlikely—that the edifice of achieved poetic intention would not, in fact, present the author with an image of his conscious poetic identity. Instead, it would reveal that identity to be only a limited and distorted part of a much larger context—a context that evades representation, yet is equally of the "self."

As an alternative to Wordsworth's complacency, Coleridge offers the recognition that the incompleteness imposed on all comprehensible order by the gap between the finite and infinite renders all utterance potentially figurative, calling the possibility of literality itself into question. Figuration thus becomes at once the substance of error—the gauge of our distance from the whole,

[11] William Wordsworth, *Poetical Works*, ed. Thomas Hutchinson (Oxford: Oxford University Press, 1971), p. 589.

literal truth—and the mode of our adaptation. The curious form of *Biographia Literaria* suggests that it is the text which provides the means of adapting figuration to truth, preventing it from enhancing self-mystification and promoting error. In *Biographia*, Coleridge assiduously avoids the kind of conclusion that implies a movement beyond the bounds of the text that provides the space in which it is possible for life and career, creator and creation, this book and other books to interact. At no point does Coleridge suggest that we are not dealing with a work in progress.

For Coleridge, figuration in general and allegorization in particular become dangerous at precisely the point at which it pretends to complete itself and become more than figurative. If we are to understand the "letter from a friend" in all its complexity, we must also recognize in it Coleridge's revision of Plato's Allegory of the Cave,[12] in which the allegory itself comes to define the nature of the cave. The gap between finite and infinite determines that we are, in effect, trapped within an allegory (or to put it another way, a figure of God's greatness) that can never be complete (and therefore, which can never validate itself) because the source of all motivation, of all design, is inaccessible. To allegorize a condition that is already allegorical is to enhance the mystery and to move farther from the truth than we already are. Nowhere in Coleridge's corpus is this more apparent than in "The Rime of the Ancient Mariner."

For these reasons, the way in which figuration is to be conceived becomes an issue extraordinarily charged with theological and philosophical significance. Coleridge had previously addressed this problem in *The Statesman's Manual* (1816):

> Now an allegory is but a translation of abstract notions into picture language which is itself nothing but an abstraction from objects of the senses; the principal being even more worthless than its phantom proxy, both alike unsubstantial, and the former shapeless to boot. On the other hand a Symbol (which is always tautegorical) is characterized by a translucence of the Special in the Individual or of the General in the Especial or of the Univer-

---

[12] Plato, *Republic*, VII.

20         sal in the General. Above all by the translucence of the
Eternal through and in the temporal. It always partakes
of the reality which it renders intelligible; and while it
enunciates the whole, abides itself as a living part in that
Unity, of which it is the representative. The others are
but empty echoes which the fancy arbitrarily associates
with apparitions of matter, less beautiful but not less
shadowy than the sloping orchard or hill-side pasture-
field seen in the lake below.   (*SM*, 30–31)

and, elsewhere, he defined allegory more precisely as:

the employment of one set of agents and images with
actions and accompaniments correspondent, so as to convey, while in disguise, either moral qualities or conceptions
of the mind that are not in themselves objects of the
senses, or other images, agents, actions, fortunes, and circumstances, so that the difference is everywhere presented
to the eye or imagination while the likeness is suggested
to the mind; and this connectedly so that the parts com-
bine to form a consistent whole.[13]

Allegory is seen by Coleridge as a consistent whole, a system of meanings embodied in a fixed set of relationships between
a literal and a figurative cosmos. The likeness between the two is
suggested to the mind while the difference is apparent to the eye
or imagination ("imagination" seems to refer here merely to the
capacity to create images). In other words, allegory depends upon
and promotes an absolute division between the qualities of a mind
inhabited by "moral qualities" and "conceptions" (including, presumably, self-conceptions) and the sensible world. By treating qualities of mind as if they were objects of the senses, allegory ultimately emphasizes the degree to which mind and meaning are not

---

[13] From an 1818 lecture, quoted in Samuel Taylor Coleridge, *Coleridge's
Miscellaneous Criticism*, ed. Thomas Middleton Raysor (Cambridge: Harvard
University Press, 1936), p. 30.

of this world. As a consequence, allegory promotes a process of self-abstraction, tending toward a sense of the mind's unreality that is, paradoxically, born of the contemplation of the mind's apparent power to create meanings out of itself more or less at will. If self-abstraction tends to emphasize the mind's unique powers, and hence to emphasize the distinctiveness of the self, by holding the world at a distance, it also raises the disturbing question, where is our substance in the world?—fueling a perpetual sense of inadequacy that is the dark underside of assertive identity.

The similarities between Coleridge's definitions of symbol and secondary imagination are too obvious to belabor. His definition of imagination is clearly aimed at establishing the internal basis for the relationship between the literal and the meaningful. What the notion of symbol adds to, or perhaps emphasizes in, his definition of secondary imagination is the way in which symbol "partakes of the reality which it renders intelligible" and "while it enunciates the whole, abides itself as a living part in that Unity." Symbol seeks to embody in the world the qualities of consciousness while maintaining a degree of distinction between them by emphasizing the degree to which the relationship remains figurative. If symbol remains a figure, it is clearly not "figurative" in any familiar tropological sense. The combination of symbol and secondary imagination is intended to intimate the sense in which understanding is itself an act of figuration, involving a trade-off between unsullied literality and pure creative will. In this context, it is easy to see that Coleridge's symbol is far less a specific kind of figure than an epistemological category coming into being—a category of mediation. It might be even more accurate to say that symbol is the means by which the question of what guarantees the validity of an act of figuration is transformed from a matter of rhetorical classification into an issue of fundamental philosophical and theological importance.

The difficulty of Coleridge's symbol, for him and for us, is in the evasiveness of its literality—the difficulty of identifying actual instances of the specifically symbolic. In his essay, "The Rhetoric of Temporality," Paul de Man questions whether the idea of the symbol ever described any actual act of Romantic figuration. De Man suggests that the true nature of Romantic figuration was disjunctive and allegorical and that, as a description of figura-

22 tive practice, the notion of the symbol was a self-deceiving mystification.[14] I think that we can appreciate de Man's rigorist point without accepting his conclusion that Coleridge was unaware that symbol was not a description of practice and without making his negative judgment on the value of the concept. But the question remains: if the intelligibility of allegory resides in the discontinuity of sight and vision, of object and idea, where does the intelligibility of symbol reside—what does it symbolize? Coleridge addresses himself to this question when he turns to the examination of the revisionary relationship between various texts, especially poems, and to the status of textuality as a mode of apprehension.

A reexamination of Coleridge's major statements on allegory will reveal that they do describe a process of figuration, taking full cognizance of its willed nature. By contrast, symbol is spoken of as if it was something discovered, not made. Rather than describing the figurative act by which the poem comes into being, it represents the qualities of the ideal text, without reference to any act of will necessary to bring it into being. If allegory is a figurative entity with interpretive implications, his symbol is an interpretive entity with implications for figuration. To put it slightly differently, symbol shifts the identity of the poem away from an act of expression that subordinates truth to will or desire and begins to regard it as an object discovered in a world of objects. This objectivity and the discipline of otherness which it implies intercepts desire and reassures us of the role of truth in the poetic act. In this sense, symbol can be viewed not as an attempt to describe poetic practice but as a revision of poetic practice, anticipating the possibility of a movement beyond the limits imposed by allegory/identity.

Coleridge's interest in subordinating other forms of figuration under the aegis of symbol reflects his concern with proving the priority of interpretation over poetic expression within the realm of phenomena conditioned by the notion of the text. This, in turn, suggests that clarifying the nature of that ontology, anticipated in the concept of the symbol, which incorporates both expression and interpretation was the implicit purpose of Coleridge's

[14] Paul de Man, "The Rhetoric of Temporality," in *Interpretation: Theory and Practice*, ed. Charles S. Singleton (Baltimore: Johns Hopkins University Press, 1969), pp. 173–209.

1815–17 endeavors. It also helps us to see how such an undertaking involves an increasing tendency to conceive of "literary" issues, like the nature of the text, as the context conditioning our perception of phenomena normally and erroneously considered extraliterary.

In any case, the letter to a friend is more than an attempt to claim for what follows something greater than it achieves. It fixes Coleridge's definitions as the object of its response and, in doing so, establishes for them a textual identity distinct from a philosophical rhetoric overcrowded with other thinkers and other ideas. The conclusion toward which we are ushered by this re-vision-by-context is that far from being the norm, the literality of language depends upon the itselfness or identity of the text, which is dependent in turn upon a self-conscious and complex figurative act.

For Coleridge, Plato's cave points out the limitations of the understanding which takes a continuous chain of ratiocination for its ideal. The limits of ratiocination confirm the legitimate role of revelation. But Plato's cave does not by itself constitute an adequate representation of our condition. We must also consider its complement, the Cave of Trophonius, into which Coleridge's friend is so reluctant to descend (*BL*, I, 200). According to the *Oxford Classical Dictionary*, Trophonius was

> apparently "the Feeder," a Boetian oracular god. . . . His oracle was held in great reverence. Pausanias . . . describes the elaborate preliminary ritual, after which the enquirer was supposed to be snatched away underground and given direct revelations.[15]

Revelation presents us with the problem of accommodat-ing it to the norm of reason—of accommodating the discontinuous to the continuity of human existence—or accepting a permanent disjunction between seer and human order, and within the identity of the seer, between the man of sight and the man of insight. The problem is particularly acute for the poet, who runs the risk of being surprised by what he has written. De Man has written of

15 *O.C.D.*, 2nd ed. (1970), p. 1097.

24　that point at which writing, as an act initiated in the will, gives way to a visitation of grace. Writing moves away from the psychological self or distinct identity which initiates it, toward the revelation of an immanent or ontological self, which is less a part of the author than a function of the rhetorical character of literary language—an attribute of the text.[16] For Coleridge, such a discontinuity at the heart of writing is a function of the larger discontinuity that makes all unrevised utterance ultimately figurative.

The poet cannot stand aloof from figuration, for it inevitably rebounds upon him. If he is to protect himself from his own poetic acts, the poet must to some degree preempt the reader's role and become the first interpreter of his own work. Indeed, this is precisely what Coleridge does in his most famous revision-by-context, the preface to "Kubla Khan."

Since Elisabeth Schneider's *Coleridge, Opium, and Kubla Khan*,[17] it has been all but impossible to accept the literal truth of Coleridge's Preface. Far from solving our problems, Schneider's book has only brought into the open the conflict between authorial denials of the poem's worth and critics' desire to take it seriously. Who does have authority over a poem already written? Does the poet's creative authority give him a special license to interpret or to preempt interpretation? The difficult relationship of preface and poem, each challenging the other's literality, raises the additional question: is literal utterance possible in the context of competing discourses?

For the critic, the preface-poem relationship presents immediately certain practical difficulties of procedure: should the poem or the preface be treated first? The poem was certainly written first, yet we come to it through the mediation of a preface

---

[16] Paul de Man, *Blindness and Insight: Essays in the Rhetoric of Contemporary Criticism* (Oxford: Oxford University Press, 1971), pp. 38–41.

[17] Elisabeth Schneider, *Coleridge, Opium, and Kubla Khan* (Chicago: University of Chicago Press, 1953). After spending hundreds of pages marshaling exhaustive medical, historical, and psychological evidence against Coleridge's claim of dream composition, Schneider admits: "The poem itself, with its essential questions, remains untouched . . ." (p. 238). Confronted with the difficulties of the poem and in spite of her determined skepticism about the rest of Coleridge's preface, she accepts at face value his contention that the poem is a fragment.

making claims that are all but impossible to ignore. The preface asserts a priority which is always, in at least one sense, false: written after, placed before, it comes between the reader and the poem as a reassertion of authorial will over its own now-externalized discourse. The preface implies Coleridge's authority to interpret as well as to create, even to interpret his own poem out of existence. The very existence of the preface suggests that the poet defines the poem, not it him. Nevertheless, the poem has its own existence in print. It stands beside and eloquently questions the pretensions of the authorial preface, inviting us to ask what it might have to say that would move Coleridge both to deny it and to print it.

Whichever beginning he chooses, the critic knows that he is already belated in relation to the claims of that other possible beginning. The indeterminate relation of preface to poem reveals the true vulnerability of poetry's claims to priority and prose's claims to literality. In practice, both poem and preface are equidistant from the literal Word. There is not, they seem to suggest, a choice to be made between poetry and prose, expression and reflection, prophecy and interpretation. Poets and critics alike must locate themselves as best they can in relation to a Word that is beyond our grasp. This mutual challenge of the authority of the poet and of his discourse reflects Coleridge's sense of the plight of consciousness trapped between self-conception—the insubstantial conviction of self—and manifestation—the concrete evidence of acts. This goes far, I think, toward explaining Coleridge's tendency, in Brisman's words, to "argue unities into dialectics."[18]

Whatever else it may be, Coleridge's preface is not a factual account of the poem's genesis.[19] Factual or not, there is no

---

18 Brisman, *Romantic Origins*, p. 36.

19 Perhaps the single most important piece of evidence against the literal truth of Coleridge's account of the composition of "Kubla Khan" is the Crewe Manuscript, discovered in 1934 in the collection of the Marquis of Crewe. The manuscript indicates that a number of minor changes were made in the manuscript of the 1816 edition. However small, these changes reflect a poet's concern with the technical quality of his work and point to the careful crafting of the rest of the poem. The degree to which the 1816 preface is a late addition to the largely finalized language of the poem is indicated by this explanatory note at the bottom of the manuscript's final page:

26   denying that the preface has had a considerable effect on the experience of reading the poem, both by its strangeness and by its insistence that a poem which would otherwise seem quite complete is in reality a fragment of a much greater and more wonderful whole now lost. The revisionary effect of the preface on the experience of the poem is undeniable, and since attempts to simply ignore it have not yielded anything approaching an adequate reading of the poem, we must ask ourselves why Coleridge put it there—what does it achieve for the experience of the poem?

In order to answer this question, we must recognize that the preface is in fact a self-conscious fiction, which constitutes an interpretation of the poem. Not only does the Crewe Note indicate that the preface was written after the language of the poem had already been more or less set, but the density of the preface fairly cries out for interpretation.

At the center of the preface is Coleridge's statement that "the images rose up before him as things, with the parallel production of the corresponding expressions, without any sensation or consciousness of effort"—he dreamed a poem. The existence of the images as "things" reminds us of the description of the primary imagination and the mind's perception of the substance of its own contents. Interestingly, we can see an analogy to this in the way that the preface treats the poem: it revises not by changing the poem itself but by placing it in a new context. The integrity of the poem as a thing is preserved, and the revision resides in what is at once an echoing, an interpreting, and a transforming of the object.

But the strangest part by far of Coleridge's account is his insistence that the expressions connected with the images of the poem rose up before him at the same time, without the sensation of effort. This represents an unexpected collapse in the boundaries separating the unconscious, spontaneous activities of the imagination (like dreaming), from the conscious, shaping activities. But

---

> This fragment with a good deal more, not recoverable, composed, in a sort of revery brought on by two grains of opium, taken to check a dysentary, at a farmhouse between Porlock and Linton, a quarter of a mile from Culbone Church, in the Fall of 1797.

A photographic reproduction of the Crewe Manuscript can be found in *The British Museum Quarterly* 26, nos. 3–4 (Spring 1963): 77–83.

what happens to the poet when the creative unconscious bypasses the creative imagination? The vision is never really his (in the sense that it is fixed and made available to the conscious mind); instead the vision possesses him (as it does in that final image in the poem of the poet in the grip of an inspired poetic madness)—he disappears into his own vision. This account links the poem on the page directly with those images as things, establishing both as objects which, for all their finish, have not yet been submitted to the revisionary faculty of imagination. This tends to establish the role of the preface as an analogue of the revisionary faculty of the secondary imagination asserting its control over the materials of the primary imagination.

But Coleridge's statement that the poem before us is incomplete complicates enormously the identification of poem with images. Once Coleridge awakens and sits down to write, he is testing the powers of the conscious, artificing imagination to recover and render what is in effect a revelation. Interestingly, the revelation at issue involves not the self's experiences of the outside world but the imagination's experience of images generated from within itself. So the poem, in the context of the preface, assumes at least three identities: as the embodiment of images in the concrete language of a poem, it represents those images that existed in Coleridge's mind as things and conveys the substance of those dream images in the experiencing; it is also the fragmented result of the imagination's attempt to fix and possess its experience; and, from the reader's point of view, it is a poem to be interpreted in its own right.

The implications of Coleridge's claim that the poem before us is a fragment go beyond the mere physical fact of its alleged incompleteness; he also implies that the experiential quality of the vision has been almost completely lost and that what remains is at best a shadow of that vision. In passing from the imagination's experience of its own contents to the imagination's possession of that experience so that it can be written down, the very feeling of the experience is changed. In gaining control over its contents, the imagination sacrifices the freshness of the original experience. The common experience to which this ultimately appeals is that shared by every writer of the painful gap between the experience of the conception in the mind and the result as it

28 exists on the page. The conception, once fixed, seems inescapably alien, no longer the possession of the imagination but a part of the world out there. Still, he recognizes it as his own, so it has an ambiguous existence as something at once "I Am" and "it is." Although something has been lost in fixing this experience, its ambiguity also gives it tremendous potential for meaning because it makes it available to revision (which is also a making visionary again).

If we consider the sequence of events suggested by the preface, this will become apparent. Coleridge had a truly amazing dream, a dream so concrete that even as he experienced it, it supplied him with correspondent expressions. But when he tried to write those expressions down, not only could he not recover the whole, but the language he did recover did not have the same meaning, or, rather, it did not mean in the same way. So, not content simply to present what he had as if it were a poem, he adds this preface which turns the text as a whole into a symbol for an altogether more amazing immanence, suggesting perhaps that only entire texts are truly symbolic and that what they symbolize is the capacity to sustain and manifest an immanence—the capacity that makes them texts. In doing so, he also manages to re-create the poem-as-object as an experience, not of vision itself but of the loss of vision. And beyond that, he is able to explore the nature and meaning of that experience. Or to speak biographically, Coleridge wrote a poem, which, either because it failed to convey the meaning he wanted it to or because it had implications he wanted to avoid (we will consider this question later), he suppressed for almost twenty years. Then, placing the poem-as-object in an entirely new context, he reopened it to new possibilities of meaning. In other words, the preface refictionalizes the fiction-become-object. This is a new, revisionary creative act which does two things at once: it shatters the poem-as-object, turning it into an open-ended fragment symbolizing meanings beyond itself; and it reverses the process by which the poem was originally created, passing back from object to experience and allowing to poet to examine the quality of his own creative experience through an act of unmaking.

Implicit in this process is a recognition that closure is a rounding off of experience that confines the possibilities of meaning

within the bounds of literary form. This is what is implied in Coleridge's view of the arbitrary character of allegory: because it is
arbitrary, things have meaning only within the context supplied
by the allegory, and the relationship between meaning inside
and outside of the allegory is shaky at best. Symbol, on the other
hand, locates the source of meaning in the objects it treats and
views literary form as an intimation of meanings that it is not entirely adequate to enclose.

But Coleridge does not simply forget the substance of his
vision; he is interrupted by the man from Porlock. On the most
immediate level, the man from Porlock seems to represent the inevitable intrusion of the outside world into the poet's enclosed,
imaginative world of the self—an intrusion that disrupts his creative state and causes the loss of his vision. Such an intrusion is
inevitable because the poet cannot escape his involvement in the
world out there any more than he can divorce his conscious from
his unconscious.

But, like the tango, business takes two—it implies com-
merce between individuals. In this sense, the business that brings
the man from Porlock into the world of the farmhouse is Coleridge's business, suggesting that the intruder also represents the
inevitable intrusion of the conscious, shaping faculty into the
workings of the poet's unconscious, dreaming imagination. The
figure of the man from Porlock argues the analogy between the
relationship of the poet's inner life with his life as a man of affairs,
and the relationship of the imagination that generates images out
of itself with the imagination that fixes them and makes them
available for revision. It also emphasizes the poet's dual role as an
"I Am" and an "it is." The poet must struggle to relate his immediate self-experience with his perception of self as object. The
means of reconciliation are his perceptions of imaginative contents
as objects.

Describing his loss of vision, Coleridge tells us: "The
rest had passed away like the images on the surface of a stream
into which a stone has been cast, but, alas! without the after restoration of the latter!" This image reminds us immediately of Coleridge's comparison of allegory to the images reflected in a lake.
This recurrent image of reflection expresses both the insubstantiality
of reality in allegory and fancy's dependence on the objects that

30 circumstance happens to put before it. The images that Coleridge dreamed were, like allegory and the fancy to which it is related, the product of an absolute division between the spontaneous, generative self and the thinking, artificing self—an absolute division of "I am" and "it is."

By writing the vision down, thus fixing it so the revisionary imagination can do its work, he gives the vision existence in the thinking, artificing self. He also suggests that the proper context of imagination is not the self but the text. When this happens, the vision is no longer the experience that divides the self absolutely but the experience that unites the self in the space defined by the text.

Analogically speaking, the same is true for the relationship between the poem and the poem-with-preface: for Coleridge the poem is the incomplete object emblematizing a self that he recognizes as his own, yet from which he feels alienated. The self that spawned the poem-as-object seems as distant from "I am" as Descartes' subject from its object. But the preface creates an echo of that poem which is completely within the bounds of the thinking, artificing self; and the intertwining of the poem and preface is the uniting of the two poems into a fragment, intimating a self beyond the normal powers of self-consciousness or representation to convey.

From the point of view of the reader, the process works in reverse: he begins with an apparently complete poem. But the preface breaks that apparent whole in order to intimate the anterior poem and the anterior levels of the self that created it. In this way, Coleridge breaks his poem so that it can mean more to the reader as a fragment than it could as a closed and complete form.

It is clear from all of this that the key to the effectiveness of the preface is its identification of the poem with the images or mental contents. Because each image is both something the mind experiences in the act of perceiving and something it peruses as object, each image is both an "I Am" and an "it is" (the experience of self versus the perception of self through the content-as-object). By establishing the analogy between the poem-as-object and the mental content-as-object, the preface establishes the identity of the poem as both "I Am" and "it is." The likeness between poem and mental content is balanced by the dissimilarity between poem-as-experience and the experiential quality of the mental contents it expresses. In this way, the preface establishes the common ground upon which an examination of the self can proceed, while maintaining our sense of the very real differences between parts of the self and between self and text.

The preface's role as transformed echo of the poem is established by the shared image of the reflection on the surface of the water, which plays a central role in each. The connection is most explicitly made when Coleridge breaks the continuity of the prose preface to quote these lines from "The Picture": "Then all the charm / Is broken—all that phantom world so fair / Vanishes, and a thousand circlets spread / And each mis-shapes the other . . ." (lines 91–94). This emphasis on the tenuous quality of the reflected image and on the distorting qualities of the reflecting surface is also at the center of the poem's lines: "The shadow of the dome of pleasure / Floated midway on the waves" (lines 31–32).

In the preface, the charm is broken when Coleridge tries to fix his vision. This attempt to fix the vision in order to possess it is the disturbance on the surface of the water that distorts and dissolves the reflected image into ripples. It is important to note that this is as much an image of transformation as of dissolution: the tenuous reflected image does dissolve, but not into nothing. It is transformed into ripples—a force propagating itself outward in concentric waves, seeking the limits of its environment. This is no bad image for the way in which the combination of preface and poem dissolves the reader's assumption of the poem's wholeness, transforming it into a series of analogies, propagating outwards to explore the limits of the creative act and its relationship to self and other.

As these ripples spread, "each mis-shapes the other." This not only confesses the inevitable distortion involved in passing from one level of analogy to another; it also implies that it is the distorting and breaking itself that provides the energy necessary to extend the initial creative-disruptive act until it fills all the space that consciousness can conceive.

Within the poem, the image of reflection is used in a quite different way: there it is used to question the status of representation. The idea of the image floating on the waves suggests the way the natural motion of the water distorts the reflected image. The

32  representation, by its very nature, distorts—even when the representation is of so direct a kind as reflection. Representation, as an extension of that part of the self which fixes and revises experience, is itself a further revision.

The image of reflection not only ties together the preface and the poem (although in each it is used to make a point peculiarly appropriate to its immediate context), it ties them both to the problem of allegorical versus the symbolic mode of representation. Using the image of reflection to describe the qualities of allegory, Coleridge is really discriminating kinds of meaning: in allegory, meaning is something that artifice arranges by its juxtaposition of literal and figurative ways of seeing—meaning is arbitrary; in symbol, meaning is seen as intimately involved with the identities of things in themselves. For example, in the first part of the image of reflection which we examined in the preface, the focus of meaning was the reflected image—something arbitrarily created by the circumstantial juxtaposition of an object with the reflecting surface. But when the disruption of the reflecting surface dissolves the image into ripples, the focus of meaning becomes the properties of the thing itself—the object before us. With the disappearance of the reflected image comes the disappearance of the absolute gap between the objective reality being contemplated and the focus of meaning. So, in this image, which is both dissolving and transformational, Coleridge enacts the passage from allegory to symbol.

The discriminations of fancy and imagination given in *Biographia* divide up the mental process into relatively static units for purposes of explanation. But as I have shown, the value of those categories resides more in the interpretation than in the application. Even there, through the strangeness of the letter from a friend, Coleridge placed the emphasis on the qualities of his formulation as an experience rather than as a statement. Quite similarly, the preface to "Kubla Khan" expresses in the strangeness of the experience that it describes the sensations of an amazed self, confronting its own imaginative processes as a mystifying other. Indeed, this is the function of the preternatural and the supernatural throughout the Mystery Poems: they keep at the center of the poetic experience the sense of confronting one's inner self as a mysterious and threatening other. This is especially so in "The Rime of the Ancient Mariner," where the mariner's inner state is projected outwards as a nightmare world of unknowable and menacing objects and events. If we think about it for a moment, we can perceive a close relationship between this experiential quality of the preface to "Kubla Khan" and Coleridge's theory of organic form. The idea that a poem generates itself from within according to an organic model expresses Coleridge's sense of the objective integrity even of the products of his own mind, once they are externalized as poems on a page. It also expresses the self's sense of its own processes operating beyond its understanding, in ways too complex to be grasped except indirectly through symbol and analogy. This dual sense of self as subject and object is the basis for Coleridge's distinction between the generative and revisionary faculties of the imagination. His emphasis on revision suggests in its turn a fundamental change in the identity of the poet: he comes to see himself not so much as the creator or generator of poems but as the prophetic reader of his own poetry. In this context, the proof of the poet's election resides not in his ability to generate poems but in his ability, in each act of poetic creation, to reenact the transformation of poet-as-creator into poet-as-reader. 🕮

# 2

"REALITY'S DARK DREAM":

The Underside of the Conversation Poems

In these next two chapters, we will be discussing how Coleridge's poetic practice provides the pretext for his theoretical formulations on allegory, symbol, and imagination and leads eventually to the contemplation of the Bible as their common point of reference. I will argue that these formulations represent Coleridge's attempt to answer the fears aroused by his own poetic practice in the Mystery and Conversation Poems and, as such, that they direct us by what they deny to those aspects of his own poetry that Coleridge found most threatening and, thus, most demanding of revision.

In his well-known essay "Structure and Style in the Greater Romantic Lyric," M. H. Abrams credited Coleridge with inventing this characteristic Romantic form and described such poems:

> They present a determinate speaker in a particularized, and usually localized, outdoor setting, whom we overhear as he carries on, in a fluent vernacular which rises easily to a more formal speech, a sustained colloquy, sometimes with himself or with the outer scene, but more frequently with a silent human auditor, present or absent. The speaker begins with a description of the landscape; an aspect or change of aspect in the landscape evokes a varied but integral process of memory, thought, anticipation, and

feeling which remains closely intervolved with the outer scene. In the course of this meditation the lyric speaker achieves an insight, faces up to a tragic loss, comes to a moral decision, or resolves an emotional problem. Often the poem rounds upon itself to end where it began, at the outer scene, but with an altered mood and deepened understanding which is the result of the intervening meditation.[1]

For our more narrowly Coleridgean purpose, we can shorten and refine this into a paradigm not literally the same as the experience described in any one Conversation Poem but which can be said to be the experience to which all of them refer.

The speaker begins with a feeling of absence, ranging in seriousness from idleness, to loss, to despair. His attention fixes on some object or event in the external scene, with which he becomes closely engaged, displacing his affect outward onto what he sees. Confronting the external world in which he has invested himself, the speaker's mind is altered by a correspondent change in his surroundings. It might be said that he escapes a moment of deepening, perhaps even dangerous (because increasingly straitened), subjectivity by "writing" his feelings onto nature, thereby objectifying self and turning nature into a kind of text of his own psyche.[2] I use the term "text" because the speaker's recovery hinges on his capacity to project more than he knows, a totality not comprehended in the conscious identity of the moment—conscious of despair, he also projects a capacity to hope; aware of isolation, he also projects a sense of community; burdened by a sense of loss, he projects a sense of life's compensatory delights. The term is also appropriate because the process of recovery is governed by a principle of exclusion: just as psychoanalysis privileges and generally limits itself to what can be uttered, the Conversation Poem turns

[1] M. H. Abrams, "Structure and Style in the Greater Romantic Lyric," in *Romanticism and Consciousness*, ed. Harold Bloom (New York: Norton, 1970), p. 201.

[2] Kenneth R. Johnston has noted that "landscape in Romantic poetry functions like the Muse of classical poetic fiction; it also functions like the text in modern critical theory" ("The Idiom of Vision," in *New Perspectives on Coleridge and Wordsworth: Selected Essays from the English Institute*, ed. Geoffrey H. Hartman [New York: Columbia University Press, 1972], p. 24).

on the possibilities and limitations of what can be projected onto the external world. In effect, the mode hopes to convince that the capacity of the world to signify, to attract meaning to itself, exceeds the capacity of self-consciousness to name or give meaning to the diversity of self-experience. Thus, the allegory of self-experience conditioned by despair, or loss, or isolation is interrupted and shown to be a part of a more inclusive, benevolent allegory. In light of our discussion in Chapter 1, it could even be said that the Conversation Poems put in the best possible light (as the Mystery Poems put in the worst possible light) the potential for the allegorizer to be allegorized in the interstices of his own allegory.

In some of the poems which will be discussed in this chapter ("The Eolian Harp," "This Lime-Tree Bower My Prison," and "Frost at Midnight"), this subjectivity that is beyond the defining capacities of allegorizing self-consciousness (identity) finds its correspondent in the perception of an immanent unity, "the Soul of each, and God of all." It is this immanence that gives nature its capacity to be meaningful and makes of the created world —man and nature alike—a vast allegory, relieving the individual consciousness of the burden of sustaining meaning by the unremitting and willful appropriation of world to self.

This paradigm raises the question of whether the transformation in the speaker's state represents a moment of mutual participation of self and other in a transcendent ontology—a metaallegory made possible by the poem but not sufficiently defined by the poetic language that gives it presence—or a purely linguistic fiction, without reference outside the play of figuration within the poem. Another way of approaching this question is to ask whether the poem itself constitutes an ontology capable of containing both the poet's desire to speak truly and to speak what he desires (by "desire" I mean that within ourselves, which Coleridge would likely have called love, that seeks to invest the not-me with a benevolent intention answering to our deepest needs and worthiest ambitions).

The Conversation Poems make tremendous demands on nature to confirm the ascendency of a benevolent order over a blind contingency not just in the world around but in the self as well. Such a level of demand presents Coleridge the poet (and us as his readers) with even more difficult questions: in what context, if any (figuration, poetry, literature, textuality, philosophy, history, religion?), is nature a fit respondent to the range and complexity of our desire? And, in what context is a subjectivity limited by identity as the primary mode of its self-awareness capable of signifying a subjectivity in which the experience of self and other are genuinely in accord and mutually encompassing? And, finally, there is the possibility, uppermost in the mind of the Coleridge of the Mystery Poems, that such demand, undisciplined by the form appropriate to it, might shatter more fragile, less encompassing conceptions of self and nature and leave him exposed to contingency alone as the dominant principle of being.

"The Eolian Harp" (1796) is an excellent example of an early Conversation Poem in which a subjective demand for the perfect expression and confirmation of an extraordinary moment of insight exceeds the signifying capacities of self and nature, leading to the negative revelation of a conflict at the heart of the poet's conception of himself. The poem begins at twilight, in a "world so hushed! / The Stilly murmur of the distant Sea / Tells us of silence" (lines 10–12). This presence so diminished from the norm as to suggest absence admits into the natural world an intense subjectivity, at once familiar and "unnatural." In this momentary absence, the speaker's attention is attracted to the Eolian harp:

> How by the desultory breeze caress'd,
> Like some coy maid half yielding to her lover,
> It pours such sweet upbraiding, as must needs
> Tempt to repeat the wrong! And now, its strings
> Boldlier swept, the long sequacious notes
> Over delicious surges sink and rise,
> Such a soft floating witchery of sound
> As twilight Elfins make, when they at eve
> Voyage on gentle gales from Fairy-Land,
> Where Melodies round honey-dropping flowers
> Footless and wild, like birds of Paradise,
> Nor pause, nor perch, hovering on untamed wing!

> (lines 14–25)

38    As soon as the mind fixes on the normally unnoticed "desultory breeze," it augments this minimal presence with its own images. The longer he listens and the more acute his awareness of the breeze becomes, the less natural are the images adequate to convey the poet's experience.

The fantastic nature of that image of elfin song, disembodied yet achieving an almost physical presence, conveys the increasingly private nature of Coleridge's experience. The figurative movement of the poem has carried him away from his initial sense of partnership with Sara, away from an awareness of the larger scene, away even from the immediate occasion of his meditation, into a rhetoric indicative of his desire for a more imaginatively satisfying, if fantastic, reality than the external world can provide.

Suddenly, we are confronted with the famous lines:

> O! the one Life within us and abroad,
> Which meets all motion and becomes its soul,
> A light in sound, a sound-like power in light
> Rhythm in all thought, and joyance everywhere—
> Methinks, it should have been impossible
> Not to love all things in a world so fill'd;
> Where the breeze warbles, and the mute still air
> Is music slumbering on her instrument.

(lines 26–33)

We are not unjustified in stopping to wonder how it is that we are brought to this startling exclamation. Clearly enough, this expression of faith is based not on the continuing presence of the world but on its progressive diminution; it is the apotheosis of that figurative movement toward a "nature" increasingly of the fancy, signaling not the meeting point of reality and desire which grants them equal validity in the context of "one Life" but the point at which desire finds its own voice—the drowning out of the "stilly murmur" and the "desultory breeze." The result is literally a

moment of *in*sight, disembodied and indeterminate in relation to
any shared experience.

As if suddenly remembering that there are others listening in, Coleridge now moves retrospectively to establish a firmer
relationship between his vision and its ostensible occasion:

> Methinks, it should have been impossible
> Not to love all things in a world so fill'd;
> Where the breeze warbles, and the mute still air
> Is music slumbering on her instrument.

(lines 30–33)

Now the vision seeks to embody itself—to assert its own reality—
by identifying its appropriate pretext in what is in fact a discontinuous act of revision.[3]

In an attempt to achieve this end more fully, the poem
goes on to normalize the privileged moment of revelation through
this explicit simile:

> And thus, my Love! as on the midway slope
> Of yonder hill I stretch my limbs at noon,
> Whil'st through my half-clos'd eye-lids I behold
> The sunbeams dance, like diamonds on the main,
> And tranquil muse upon tranquility;
> Full many a thought uncall'd and undetain'd,
> And many idle flitting phantasies,
> Traverse my indolent and passive brain
> As wild and various as the random gales
> That swell and flutter on this subject Lute.

(lines 34–43)

[3] Geoffrey Hartman remarks in a discussion of "Hymn Before Sunrise, in
the Vale of Chamouni" that "several stills . . . or re-visions relax the hold
of a spell that almost paralyzed the soul" ("Evening Star and Evening Land,"
in *The Fate of Reading and Other Essays* [Chicago: University of Chicago
Press, 1975], p. 172).

40 But this simile, emphasizing the passivity and arbitrariness that the idle brain of the poet shares with the harp, is no adequate occasion for the confident and vigorous assertion of the earlier lines. Already the immediacy of that moment is diminishing, and the play of figures—harp, wind, idle brain, flitting fantasy—is adequate only to sustain a question which is, by implication, still another of those idle speculations:

> And what if all of animated nature
> Be but organic Harps diversely fram'd,
> That tremble into thought, as o'er them sweeps
> Plastic and vast, one intellectual breeze,
> At once the Soul of each, and God of all?

> (lines 44–48)

What has been lost is that sense of being infused, of identifying with a quickening power. Now, the poet is with nature, awaiting (not too seriously) the visitation of that awakening force.

In the final sixteen lines, the poem abandons completely the notion of the "one Life," immanent in self and nature, in favor of "him / The incomprehensible!" ostensibly in response to Sara's reproof. Contrary to what this implies, the failure of the poem is not due to a failure of humility or an inability to remain properly open and receptive; it is due to a failure of the active imagination to overcome the limits of Coleridge's individual identity and imagine, through himself, a more generous, less burdened subjectivity. Whether we see it as a failure of imaginative nerve or as a suitable reintegration with the larger, if limited, community of men, the self-description of the final lines reveals the anxiety, the lack of a sense of the self's legitimacy in the world, that has been present from the poem's opening lines, when Coleridge first mused upon the wife and home of which he feels himself to be unworthy.

The reading of this poem is somewhat complicated by an extensive history of revision. If, for example, we remove the "one Life" passage—a later addition (first appearing in the errata to *Sibylline Leaves*), emphasizing the discontinuity between the priv-

ileged moment of insight and its occasion in the external world—
we can see more clearly the original's emphasis on the poet's failure to translate his own subjectivity into a vision of the "one intellectual breeze." The translation of mere fancy into real conviction
is blocked by his anxiety over the perceived disjunction between
his sinful nature and his good fortune. It is Coleridge's own inner
division that decrees that the unity immanent in the created world
remain "incomprehensible." Without the "one Life" passage, we
would not have so clear a sense of the precise nature of the moment
that the rest of the poem fails to support. Thus, even as it makes
the poem more satisfyingly dramatic, Coleridge's revision makes
clear the precise nature of the poem's failure (and Coleridge's own
awareness of the problem).

Apparently, he did make a serious attempt to make the
poem work in 1803, when he removed the obtrusively fanciful lines
(21–25) about "twilight Elfins," "Fairy-land," and "Melodies . . .
hovering on untam'd wing." In this revision, tentative speculations
about the "one intellectual breeze" are immediately preceded by
their occasioning images of the harp and the poet lying idle on a
hillside. Although it serves to tighten somewhat the figurative
logic of the poem, this version does nothing to narrow the gap between the poet's own divided subjectivity and the unified subjectivity that he seeks to envision.

The *Sibylline Leaves* version of the poem, with this passage restored and the "one Life" passage added, reflects Coleridge's
conviction of the intimate relationship between the inadequacies of
identity and the limitations of figuration. "The Eolian Harp," as
Coleridge's revisions suggest he came to understand it, founders on
his inability to distinguish clearly his subjectivity from its most obtrusive expression, his divided identity, so that it could serve not
just as a metaphor, expressing his desire for confirmation of consciousness' place in the world (as a part of God's immanent subjectivity) but as an analogue expressing the truth of the vision as
well.

Written in 1797, "This Lime-Tree Bower My Prison"
was revised (without, I think, much effect on its meaning) and first
published in 1800. The poem demonstrates a more effective strategy
than the simple renunciation of "The Eolian Harp" for intercepting
the poem's movement beyond the limits of natural order into pure

42 subjectivity. This new strategy, which I will call "bestowal," involves a substantial break in the logic of the poem, but it also denies the necessity of choosing between the figurative and the real, the privileged and the shared experience.

At the beginning of the poem, Coleridge sits alone in his garden, musing on the "Beauties and feelings, such as would have been / Most sweet to my remembrance even when age / Had dimm'd mine eyes to blindness!" (lines 3–5). He begins to fill the emptiness occasioned by this sense of loss by imagining the course of his friends' wanderings over a familiar landscape. This imagined progress soon becomes an invocation of nature's greatest splendors on behalf of "My gentle-hearted Charles," who "hast pined / And hunger'd after Nature, many a year / In the great City pent" (lines 28–30):

> . . . Ah! slowly sink
> Behind the western ridge, thou glorious Sun!
> Shine in the slant beams of the sinking orb,
> Ye purple heath-flowers! richlier burn, ye clouds!
> Live in the yellow light, ye distant groves!
> And kindle, thou blue Ocean! So my friend
> Struck with deep joy may stand, as I have stood,
> Silent with swimming sense; yea gazing round
> On the wide landscape, gaze till all doth seem
> Less gross than bodily; and of such hues
> As veil the Almighty Spirit, when yet he makes
> Spirits perceive his presence.

(lines 32–43)

Coleridge's engagement with nature here is an imaginary one, aimed less at remedying his own sense of loss than tending toward a spontaneous bestowal of his own most intense experience of the natural world. The culmination of this subjective experience is the apprehension in the elements of the natural scene of their common manifestation of the "Almighty Spirit."

This act of bestowal is an expression of love of community

reaching toward a shared ground of experience and, hence, of thought and feeling. It is important to recognize, however, that the privileged moment of revelation is kept at a distance; it is only recalled by the poet and is bestowed imaginatively. There is the suggestion here that the very tenuousness of the bestowal's status as an act or event is necessary to prevent it from being caught up (along with the poem as a whole) in the isolating logic of the privileged moment to which it refers.

Coleridge's spontaneous and loving gesture releases him from his feeling of loss and confinement, and infused with a new sense of fullness, he turns appreciatively to his own immediate surroundings. He now realizes that "nature" is everywhere; it is not limited by the logic of inclusion/exclusion or of desire-intercepted-by-limitation that governs his own identity-burdened consciousness: "Henceforth I shall know / That Nature ne'er deserts the wise and pure; / No plot so narrow, be but Nature there" (lines 59–61).

The bower is a prison only insofar as the poet has imposed this figurative logic on nature. But now he is ostensibly freed from the straitening logic of his distinct identity to envision a meeting and greeting based on the two friends' common participation in a ubiquitous nature:

> My gentle-hearted Charles! when the last rook
> Beat its straight path along the dusky air
> Homewards, I blest it! deeming its black wing
> (Now a dim speck, now vanishing in light)
> Had cross'd the mighty Orb's dilated glory,
> While thou stood'st gazing. . . .
>
> (lines 69–74)

This is the actual revelation toward which the poem moves: that nature—its sights, sounds, and smells—is privileged because it provides that level of experience shared by all which serves as the basis for the conviction that there is among men a community of thought and feeling. It is this community of the subjective rather than the unity (elusive indeed) of the individual

44 identity which provides, in this poem, the faith that sustains a vision of an immanent Almighty Spirit.

The sun is the element in Coleridge's imagined account of Lamb's walk, which is, in fact, present in the scene surveyed by both men. As such, it becomes the concrete reality binding together two men who live, as all of us do, by busily projecting themselves on the world around. Coleridge's isolation in the garden may, perhaps fancifully, be seen as his imprisonment in the realm of figuration conditioned by his willful imposition of his desire on the rest of the world. He is released from this imprisonment by a coincidence of willfulness and selflessness which allows him to recognize the presence of a shared nature, with an existence beyond the meanings that we give it and the identity-confirming satisfactions that we seek from it.

In many ways, this is the most comforting of the Conversation Poems. Nevertheless, its success is based largely on a skillful evasion of some of the most disturbing questions raised by the mode. The transformation in the poet's mood ("A delight / Comes sudden on my heart, and I am glad / As I myself were there!") seems to take as its occasion the vision of the "Almighty Spirit" that immediately precedes it. Yet that vision is legitimized in the poem not by the poet's capacity to give presence to and sustain the voice proper to such a vision (as in the "one Life" passage) but by the fact that it is not for himself that Coleridge seeks revelation. He is careful indeed to keep the privileged insight at an imaginative and temporal distance, thus avoiding the risk involved in submitting it to the present moment of the poem. Despite the fact that his demand takes the form of a bestowal, it nonetheless leaves us with the question of whether the revelation is an expression of a truth perceived or merely of a desire to escape the burden of the subjective.

The coincidence of a willful act with a selfless purpose obscures the true nature of the discontinuity between the change in the speaker's mood and its supposed occasion. The fact that it is involved with an act of bestowal is offered in place of any real context for the meeting and greeting of the Almighty. The implication is that the manifestation of this spirit immanent in nature is only a figure, a measure of the intensity of the speaker's engagement with and demand upon nature and upon other people.

In "The Eolian Harp," the immediate presence of Sara serves, superficially at least, to turn Coleridge away from his pursuit of visionary insight. It should be noted that the acts of bestowal that are so intimately involved with the apparently successful resolutions of "This Lime-Tree Bower My Prison," "The Nightingale," "Frost at Midnight," and "Dejection" depend not upon the intimate presence but upon the absence or silence of the other person. Neither the notoriously urban Lamb nor the lady of "Dejection," and certainly not the speechless or sleeping babies of "The Nightingale" and "Frost at Midnight" can be given the opportunity to deny that what they want and what Coleridge most wants for them are one and the same. Just as identity holds the world at bay, keeping intact the self's defensive sense of its own distinctiveness, these acts of bestowal stand between the poet and the demands that others might make on him, guaranteeing that his interaction with them is carried out in terms of what he most desires and most avidly seeks.

The point of insisting on the degree of deception involved in the positive tone of the Conversation Poems is not to reveal Coleridge's secret Machiavellianism nor to suggest that he is not a good poet—both the idealism and the poetry are genuine enough. The poetry finally acts to dissemble the excessive level of Coleridge's demands on nature and on individual human companionship because those desires involve an excessive demand on the capacities of poetry itself. It may be useful to say that the poetry itself must dissemble, despite the sincerity of the man, in order to remain poetry—to preserve its own formal identity.

The problem remains that in "This Lime-Tree Bower My Prison" there exists no language to articulate the process by which the figure of the Almighty Spirit is translated into the actual change in the poet's state of mind. Nevertheless, the poem depends on some private, subjective event that occurs in this discontinuous ground between figure and act. Thus, the poem finally depends on an implicit event that escapes the order of nature, escapes the order of figuration, and escapes even the order of the self.

But before examining in "Dejection" the ultimate implications of Coleridge's dependence on the sudden and contingent eruption of "delight" to counter the effects of identity's defensive demands on the world, I want to take a look at "The Nightingale."

46 Written in 1798, this poem intimates that under the unremitting pressure of human demand, the loss of nature's literality is a cumulative, historical process, from which it may be too late to withdraw. The poem experiments with the possibility of reversing the effects of figuration as an instrument of demand in order to experience nature in an unmediated form.

When the nightingale's song breaks in upon the poet's injunction, "let us think upon the vernal showers" (line 9), he responds spontaneously in terms of Milton's line from "Il Penseroso": "And hark! the Nightingale begins its song, / 'Most musical, most melancholy' bird!" (lines 12–13). Prepared perhaps by the mood of twilight abeyance in which the poem begins, the poet immediately becomes aware of what he has done and rebels against this automatic projection of literary experience onto the natural scene:

> A Melancholy bird? Oh! idle thought!
> In nature there is nothing melancholy.
> But some night-wandering man whose heart was pierced
> With the remembrance of a grievous wrong,
> Or slow distemper, or neglected love,
> (And so, poor wretch! filled all things with himself,
> And made all gentle sounds tell back the tale
> Of his own sorrow) he, and such as he,
> First named these notes a melancholy strain.
> And many a poet echoes the conceit.
>
> (lines 14–23)

Coleridge's immediate response to the nightingale is a revelation to himself of the degree to which our responses—those responses that seem most spontaneous, and hence most natural—are projections of states of mind thoroughly conditioned, perhaps even created, by literary and textual models. On the other hand, the self-consciousness involved in using a *Miltonic* line also brings an awareness of what he is doing and a new determination to avoid projection, signaled by "In nature there is nothing melancholy."[4]

---

[4] In *Lyrical Ballads* (1798 and 1800) and in *Sibylline Leaves* (1817), Coleridge includes a note to line 13:

There is an implicit distinction of great importance being made
here between simple displacement or projection of affect and a
"textualizing" of the world which is at once a vehicle of subjective
demand and a means of imposing a discipline of awareness on that
demand. In the case of the "night-wandering man," who "filled
all things with himself," the capacity of nature to signify is limited
by individual identity. But in limiting the diversity of nature within the confines of self-awareness, man also limits the possibilities
of his own subjectivity: he becomes sufficiently defined by a melancholy which he is unable to control, and he can find no confirmation in the external world of an identity distinct from that melancholy. Even worse, his melancholy becomes a sufficient definition
of the external world as well, and thus a contingent emotional
state subsumes both man and nature into itself.

   The figure of the melancholy man is also interesting because it introduces a new element into the problematic of the Conversation Poems—an intimation of the perversity of desire. Man's
demand here for confirmation, for a place in the world appropriate to him, appears as completely distinct from any logic of self-
interest—from the tenuous controls imposed by the notion that
desire is desire for something. In "The Nightingale," not only figuration but poetry as well is motivated by desire and governed by
demand. But that motivation continues to elude controlling forms,
remaining a principle of radical contingency at the heart of any
imaginative, created order.

   Fortunately, the poem seems to suggest, the textual models

---

   This passage in Milton possesses an excellence far superior to that
   of mere description; it is spoken in the character of the melancholy
   Man, and has therefore a *dramatic* propriety. The author makes
   this remark to rescue himself from the charge of having alluded
   with levity to a line in Milton; a charge than which none could be
   more painful to him, except perhaps that of having ridiculed his
   Bible. (*Poetical Works*, I, 264)

Of course the mere existence of the note emphasizes the reference, but it also
clearly exonerates Milton from the faults of the "night-wandering man" and
the lesser poets. Most important is Coleridge's explicit comparison of the significance of Milton's poetry with that of the Bible. The note is almost prophetic, for, as we shall see, the problem of identifying the grounds upon which
Milton and the Bible can share the same significant role is soon to become
crucial.

48 mediate between demand and reality, confronting the self with an objective image of the contingency which drives it and thus enabling it to bring demand back under control. Functioning within the context not just of a figuration easily subverted by desire but of specific textuality as well, demand is prevented from requiring more than the natural order can provide. The implication, quickly borne out a few lines later, is that nature cannot retain its literality without textual mediation.

Now Coleridge turns aside briefly to criticize those poets who have echoed the night-wandering man's "conceit." These poets, refusing to submit themselves to the discipline of the text or to seeing the world clearly, have moved too far from the literality of the natural world. These poets intimate still another distinction, this time between general and specific textuality. There is a suggestion that limiting the concept of the text to specific models results in the establishing of fixed relationships between the elements of nature and subjective states. These relationships, once fixed, limit and condition the possible ways of experiencing both self and nature. In its ultimate implications, special textuality is entropic, using up the external world and, in doing so, increasingly circumscribing response. By contrast, a general textuality is based on a knowledge of a number of texts, no one of which is sufficient to define textuality. In this context, the relationships between natural objects or events and self-experience are fixed only conditionally. The possibility of distinguishing the natural reality from its figurative use, even within the bounds of the text, makes general textuality antientropic. But after this mere hint in the direction of a broader textuality, Coleridge turns away in pursuit of the detextualization of nature—an attempt to step outside figuration and respond with an open mind and heart:

> My Friend, and thou, our Sister! we have learnt
> A different lore: we may not thus profane
> Nature's sweet voices, always full of love
> And joyance! 'Tis the merry Nightingale
> That crowds, and hurries, and precipitates
> With fast thick warble his delicious notes,
> As he were fearful that an April night

Would be too short for him to utter forth
His love-chant, and disburthen his full soul
Of all its music!

(lines 40–48)

This attempt to set aside mediation runs into trouble immediately. Not only is the nightingale perceived as a representative of a nature that is full of "love and joyance," but the bird himself has a "love chant," "a full soul," and sings "as he were fearful." Ironically, the more the poet strains to express directly his meaning, that is, to convey his immediate response to the experience of the nightingale, the more recourse he must take to figurative language and projection. And in the absence of some kind of controlling fictional form within which figuration can operate, the willed nature of the figuration becomes increasingly intrusive, making the poem sound forced. The disappearance of textual mediation serves to make the indirectness of experience even more palpable, and there is even some question of whether the bird is not less real than before. In addition, the same critique which calls into question the assertion that the nightingale is melancholy is equally destructive of Coleridge's counterassertion that nature is full of love and joyance. Within the realm of figurative language, there is no ground for proving one view superior to the other: they are equally valid as acts of figuration, and equally questionable as statements of truth.

The poet's response to this recognition is the refictionalizing of his meaning: he recasts it in a circumstantial context, based on the implicit contrast between the deserted castle of the great lord, with its overgrown gardens, and the gentle maid who is the self-effacing witness to nature as it exists when the impositions of human edifice/artifice are withdrawn. The lord and the castle may remind us slightly of Kubla Khan and his pleasure dome, especially as the lord's absence and the ruin of the castle suggest the withdrawal of human forms from a natural space which the nightingales have reinhabited. The simplicity of the maid's "hospitable home" indicates the self-effacing receptiveness which allows her to observe the nightingales without disrupting their

50 natural behavior. Within this context, Coleridge continues to approach his meaning through a self-consciously figurative language, and, as a result, the inevitable displacements of affect are less intrusive.

The attempt to dispense with mediation brings us face to face not with the nightingale but with the indispensability of projection or displacement if meaning is to be achieved.[5] As a signifier, the bird is initially overwhelmed by the subjective signified. The introduction of a more circumstantial fiction provides a scene, a second nature, inhabited by a number of signifiers, no one of which bears the entire weight of the signified. This fictionalization reflects an implicit recognition of the distinction between figuration and textualization, for it involves the contextualization of the figurative act, resisting the tendency of the will to impose its own psychologically contingent demand of the moment on the identity of the self or on the identity of nature.

This part of the poem culminates in two images of the nightingales' behavior. In the first, all the birds fall silent as a passing cloud obscures the moon, and then all begin singing again at the very moment the moon reappears. In the second, the nightingale tunes his song to the rhythm of his perch swinging in the wind. These images point to a fundamental accord between the various elements of the natural world and imply through the figure of the maid that it is at least possible for man to participate in this accord. This is a revelation of the priority of natural order over natural contingency. If, like the maid, we can suspend our urge to control and to displace, we can apprehend this order by view-

---

[5] Hartman has argued that Coleridge's imagination sees itself as inherently secondary not only because he follows great poetical and philosophical precursors but primarily because of the one precursor, the primary imagination. According to Hartman, "His religious sensibility, conspiring with a burdened personal situation, makes him feel at a hopeless remove from originality" ("Evening Star and Evening Land," p. 167). In this poem, Coleridge is discovering that his secondariness is not a question of his precursors' shadows but is inherent—a recognition comprehended in his formulations concerning primary imagination and allegory. It should be pointed out, however, that these formulations also redefine secondariness as a trait away from Coleridge as an individual and identify it as more or less characteristic of all postbiblical texts. There is some question as to whether secondariness is so much the cause of Coleridge's poetic difficulties as a retrospective formulation by which he brought certain psychological events associated with his poetic failure under control and objectified them as intellectual problems.

ing nature from within. If we view it from without, seeing nature as the lord does in terms of what we can build upon it or of its resistance to our wishes, it seems fragmented and given over to contingency.

But this revelation of order in nature also creates a certain perplexity, for it raises the question of whether a perceived unity, within a poem for example, is not in fact ultimately dependent upon a lack of knowledge, upon an artificially limited perspective, and not a revelation of fundamental truth at all. It is from this implication that the poem turns in one of those sharp changes in direction with which we have become so familiar in Coleridge's Conversation Poems. "Farewell!" (line 87) signals a new distance from the fiction he has been developing, which effectively intercepts the movement of the poem toward a radical questioning of the meaning it seeks to express.

From the "gentle Maid" and the lord of the castle, Coleridge shifts his focus to the figure of "My dear babe" (line 91). The child is "capable of no articulate sound" (line 92), which is to say that he has not yet learned to impose himself on the world through the instrument of language. That this is one of the consequences of language is suggested by the fact that he *is* old enough to "Mar all things with his imitative lisp" (line 93). It is because the child's use of language is unskilled that he can be *seen* to mar things through speech, but the implication is not that when he grows up he will cease to do so but that his use of language will become sufficiently skilled that its effects will no longer be apparent.

Because he has not yet been incorporated into the adult world, Coleridge's son can respond spontaneously, without mediation, to the world around. Ostensibly, the transition to the figure of the baby extricates Coleridge's meaning from the fictional context in which it was developed and places it firmly in the context of the familiar and, hence, of the real.

The problem is that while the figure of the maid suggests at least the possibility of adult openness to nature, the transferring of this idea out of the realm of the frankly fictional requires recourse to the figure of the child—an undeveloped and prelinguistic consciousness. The conclusion to which we are led, willy-nilly, is that mature consciousness inevitably distorts nature and mediates all experience in the image of its own desire. The instrument of the distortion is language, which, by usurping the role of nature, becomes the source of our power even as it commits us permanently to reside within the realm of mediation.

The poem's ending, another act of bestowal, in which Coleridge promises to expose his child to nature and to encourage the spontaneity of his responses, is, in its upbeat tone, a rhetorical repression of the implications we have recognized in the differences between the figures of the maid and the babe, between the success of the fiction on its own terms, and its limitations in terms of the nonfictional world.

As early as "Frost at Midnight" (1798) Coleridge had begun to inject into the Conversation Poems the idea that we receive from nature only what we bestow. In that poem, he says of the "stranger":

> Methinks, its motion in this hush of nature
> Gives it dim sympathies with me who live,
> Making it a companionable form,
> Whose puny flaps and freaks the idling Spirit
> By its own moods interprets, every where
> Echo or mirror, seeking of itself,
> And makes a toy of Thought.
>
> (lines 17–23)

In "Frost at Midnight," the idea that the world is "a toy of thought" does not prevent a final statement of faith in nature's role as:

> The lovely shapes and sounds intelligible
> Of that eternal language, which thy God
> Utters, who from eternity doth teach
> Himself in all, and all things in himself.
> Great universal Teacher! he shall mould
> Thy spirit, and by giving make it ask.
>
> (lines 59–64)

The presence of both these views in the poem suggests that Coleridge is coming around to the view that our ability to see in nature an "eternal language" and to understand it rightly depends upon something within ourselves predisposing us to do so. Without this predisposition, nature would be dead to us.

In connection with this view, there is a subtle shift in emphasis in the poetry away from the transformative and therapeutic properties of nature to an anxiety about the continued survival of that within the self which imaginatively transforms nature into the eternal language of God. This anxiety achieves its most complete expression in the 1802 poem "Dejection." At the beginning of the poem, the speaker, listening to "the dull sobbing draft, that moans and rakes / Upon the strings of this Aeolian lute / Which better far were mute" (lines 6–8), sees evidence of a coming storm and looks forward to:

> The coming on of rain and squally blast.
> And oh! that even now the gust were swelling,
> And the slant night-shower driving loud and fast!
> Those sounds which oft have raised me, whilst they awed,
> And sent my soul abroad,
> Might now perhaps their wonted impulse give,
> Might startle this dull pain, and make it move and live!
>
> (lines 14–20)

The poem begins with the dejected poet, feeling only "dull pain," calling upon the quickening forces of nature to quicken him as well. But as the two "mights" which begin the final lines of the first movement suggest, the poet seems to have lost his faith in the reality of nature's power to overcome so deep a dejection as this.

In Part II, the poet goes more deeply into the quality of his dejection, "A stifled, drowsy, unimpassioned grief, / Which finds no natural outlet, no relief, / In word, or sign, or tear—" (lines 21–24), and goes on to lament that he has lost the power to feel, rather than simply see, how beautiful his natural surroundings are.

Then, in Part III, he rejects the possibility that natural

54 violence may succeed where natural beauty failed and concludes: "I may not hope from outward forms to win / The passion and the life, whose fountains are within" (lines 45–46). Joy, the poet tells us, is "this strong music in the soul" (line 60). There was a time when joy was stronger within him than affliction, but now:

> . . . each visitation
> Suspends what nature gave me at my birth,
> My shaping spirit of Imagination.
> For not to think of what I needs must feel,
> But to be still and patient, all I can;
> And haply by abstruse research to steal
> From my own nature all the natural man—
> This was my sole resource, my only plan:
> Till that which suits a part infects the whole,
> And now is almost grown the habit of my soul.
>
> (lines 84–93)

The first thing we notice is that the lines give priority to joy over imagination presumably because only joy can counter the despair that defeats imagination's "shaping spirit." According to Coleridge, his "sole resource" was to endure his dejection while trying by means of "abstruse research" to fix, to define, to delimit himself—to erect an identity, an abstraction of himself, capable of defending against the contingencies that are equally a part of the "natural man's" experience of himself. Erecting this identity into an adequate definition of the whole, Coleridge has succeeded only in creating a mystified, almost demonic complement to his acknowledged self. Now, what has been repressed or has not been appropriated to self-definition emerges as a contingency that overwhelms. The prisoner of a self-created mystery—a demonic parody of poetic inspiration—the poet suffers not only the subjugation of his creative and thinking selves but of the world as well. For what the divided poet finally has to bestow is the curse of his own division, the demonic quality of his own returned repressions. What nature has to offer the Coleridge of "Dejection" is not the revelation of an immanent, divine subjectivity but an unmercifully accurate reflection of the qualities of consciousness as an act performed on the world.

The end of Part VI is the nadir of the poet's spirits in the poem, but the beginning of Part VII initiates a reversal startling in its apparent arbitrariness and radical discontinuousness from what has gone before:

> Hence, viper thoughts, that coil around my mind.
>     Reality's dark dream!
> I turn from you, and listen to the wind,
> Which long has raved unnoticed. What a scream
> Of agony by torture lengthened out
> That lute sent forth! . . .

(lines 94–99)

The phrase "Reality's dark dream" places Coleridge's troubling reflections in a strange relationship with the rest of experience, implying ambiguously both that they are the substance of reality, which can only be characterized as a dark dream, and that they are the underside of reality—the dark dream complementing the apprehension of the real. Even more interesting, however, is the suggestion that not the "viper thoughts" but mind itself is reality's dark dream, generating out of itself a dreamlike, distorted, and ultimately self-referential "reality."

It is apparently the "scream" of the Eolian harp that distracts the poet from his revery, returning us not just to the beginning of the poem, where a "dull sobbing draft" raked the strings, but to the beginnings of the Conversation Poems as a mode and as a period of Coleridge's career. The very arbitrariness of the meaning previously attached to the lute is revealed, and instead of a figure promoting a sense of the unity immanent in creation, the lute becomes an image of the contingency governing the self and the world created out of that self. The "scream" that snaps the poet's revery is thus his own scream, temporarily easing the pressure—the voice proper to the moment. Indeed, he protests against

56  the feelings, unrecognized and uncontrolled, that play over the fragile instrument of the self he has created:

> . . . Thou wind, that rav'st without,
>   Bare crag, or mountain-tarn, or blasted tree,
> Or pine-grove whither woodman never clomb,
> Or lonely house, long held the witches home,
>   Methinks were fitter instruments for thee.
>
> (lines 99–103)

The changing relationship between wind and lute denies that there is a stable, necessary connection between the external world and any meaning. Figuration is just figuration, and reality is no respecter of imagistic propriety. The revelation of the arbitrariness at the heart of a figure representative of Coleridge's faith that there is a metaallegory, guaranteeing the reality of representation, linking self and nature in an ultimate order, has grave consequences for self-understanding. For if the poet is the harp, the instrument of identity, he is also the wind. And the arbitrary relationship between the two signals a new sense of the arbitrariness and conflict at the center of self-representation. What is finally represented is an unbridgeable gap between self-experience and self-understanding.

The poem continues:

> Mad Lutanist! who in this month of showers,
> Of dark-brown gardens and of peeping flowers,
> Mak'st Devil's yule, with worse than wintry song,
> The blossoms, buds, and timorous leaves among.
>   Thou Actor! perfect in all tragic sounds!
> Thou Mighty Poet, e'en to frenzy bold!
>
> (lines 104–109)

This violent wind, making "worse than wintry" song in what is supposed to be a temperate month, now becomes the creative demand that is still another, perhaps the greatest, contingency in the poet's otherwise orderly and benign "nature" ("gardens of peeping flowers . . . The blossoms, buds, and timorous flowers among"). Assaulting, confusing, ravaging, and appropriating to itself one guise then another, the "Mighty Poet" within drives the man before him. The demand that Coleridge makes on the world is only a shadow of the demand he makes on himself to confirm and fulfill a limitless need (I am tempted to call it an ambition to appropriate)—a need that quite possibly exceeds the fulfilling capacities of self and of nature. This movement of the poem culminates in a kind of personal apocalypse—the rout of the old order of the self that leaves in its wake a hush and, with the realization that "all is over," a new expectancy which finds expression in another tale "of less afright, / And tempered with delight / As Otway's self had framed the tender lay":


> What tell'st thou now about?
> 'Tis of the rushing of an host in rout,
> With groans, of trampled men, with smarting wounds—
> At once they groan with pain, and shudder with the cold!
> But hush! there is a pause of deepest silence!
> And all that noise, as of a rushing crowd,
> With groans and tremulous shudderings—all is over—
> It tells another tale, with sounds deep and loud!
> A tale of less afright,
> And tempered with delight,
> As Otway's self had framed the tender lay,—
> 'Tis of a little child
> Upon a lonesome wild,
> Not far from home, but she hath lost her way:
> And now moans low in bitter grief and fear,
> And now screams loud, and hopes to make her mother hear.

(lines 110–125)


There is a grief here, born of a sense of dislocation and loss, yet there is also delight—first at the conviction that home is somewhere nearby; and, second, and perhaps most importantly, at the sense of being reborn to see the world anew through childish eyes. There are children at the ends of "The Nightingale" and "Frost at Midnight"—magical figures of limitless potential and unburdened perception—who serve as alter egos, embodying qualities desired but which Coleridge has not the boldness or strength to claim for himself except as their pro(pre?)genitor. Here Coleridge comes closest to becoming a child himself. In exchange for that renewed perception of himself and the world, he is now willing to accept the burden of the child's reality—a femaleness that no longer insists on imprinting his will on the world by having (or being) a son. In the context of this renunciation, at once more genuine and more vexing than that of "The Eolian Harp," he offers what may be the most genuinely unselfish of the many blessings that he bestows in his poetry—a blessing which must, for the moment, stand in surety for the rebirth intimated, the coming home not yet achieved, at the end of Part VII.

The "Dejection" poet subjects himself to tremendous pressures, which he successfully, if precariously, prevents from destroying him. He is not able to erect any permanent defense against them either—he remains exposed to the return of all that has been repressed in order to make possible his poetic identity and the poetry that confirms it. And although poetry and its figurative instruments have finally been able to contain this eruption of the contingent, their capacity to justify themselves as vehicles of truth and to articulate from within the evidence of their own value has been decisively compromised. Poetry and figuration work, but they neither explain nor justify themselves.

The figure of the army in rout signals the final defeat of figuration, as an instrument of orderly self and other representation, in repressing that apocalyptic desire that is at the root of the desire to be a poet. Neither the self nor nature is finally adequate to support the representation of the vast and encompassing immanence that is alone sufficient to answer and balance out that demand. The "one Life," the "Almighty Spirit," and the other immanences of the earlier poems do not finally escape the limitations of *self*-representation. They are too dependent for their substance on a nature already tamed to the demands of self, and too dependent for their inwardness on a burdened and divided identity.

By 1802 and "Dejection," Coleridge is frankly acknowledging not only the degree to which emotional contingency is threatening to evade personal and poetic controls, but he is also contemplating the possibility that the tenuous equilibrium between dejection and joy may tip permanently in the direction of dejection. In both "The Nightingale" and "Dejection," references to specific poets like Milton and even Otway help to reassert the priority of the poem over the contingencies motivating the man to write, intimating that literary awareness functions at a level equal to or perhaps greater than that of other primary modes of apprehension. But in both cases, it remains merely an invoking of something dimly apprehended beyond the ordering limits of the individual poem, of nature, or of the self. In these Conversation Poems, Milton and Otway are quite literally names to conjure with. But even though these invocations are benevolent in the short run, they too are potentially damaging to Coleridge's sense of himself as a poet— in the first case, because through Milton he implies his reservations about Wordsworth's treatment of nature, while evading the acid test of his own muse in a struggle for priority that he is clearly not confident of winning; in the second case, because in the moment of crisis, he grasps at an image whose regenerative powers have been established poetically not by Otway but by Wordsworth.[6]

What the Conversation Poems do succeed in establishing is a correspondence between the contingent demand that informs the act of writing and the poet's failure to articulate those subjective events, residing in the discontinuity of body and conclusion, that compromise the figurative logic of the poems. Although the Conversation Poems generally succeed in presenting the results of their own arbitrariness in a favorable light, they provide no basis for believing that this is inherently so. Thus, the poems become revelations to the poet of his own imperfect understanding of the relationship between his conscious intention and the intentionality manifested in his poems. There is at least the potential here, realized in the Mystery Poems, for an increasingly alienated and anxiety-ridden relationship between poet and poem. What Coleridge approaches is not a confirmation that imagination, will, and desire

[6] For more on Coleridge's troubled relationship with his precursors, especially Milton and Wordsworth, see Harold Bloom, "Coleridge: The Anxiety of Influence," in *New Perspectives on Coleridge and Wordsworth*, pp. 247–67.

60 are legitimate and integral parts of the natural world but a negative revelation that they are anomalies—contingencies disrupting the serenity of an orderly creation. The poetry most closely associated with this negative revelation—a poetry less of the immanent than of the unconscious—is found in the Mystery Poems, to which we now turn. ❈

# 3

## THE PROPHETIC READER
## AND THE PSYCHOLOGICALLY
## CONTINGENT:

### The Mystery Poems

The role of the prophetic reader as an indication of the limits of the lyric form and as a rejection of the fate of the visionary poet finds its origins in the self-revisions of the Mystery Poems: in the relationship between "Kubla Khan" and its preface; between "The Rime of the Ancient Mariner" and its gloss; and between "Christabel" and its "Conclusion to Part II." These poems reveal that there is no necessity in the alliance of figuration with conscious identity nor with any other constructed order. Committing himself to what he believes initially to be a poetic order, corresponding to the orders of self and nature, Coleridge finds himself implicated in a figurative world manipulated from within his own most powerful repressions. Thus, the alienation of the poet from his poetry becomes the central fact of poetic creation.

Although it was not the earliest of the Mystery Poems, "Christabel" seems the most logical place to begin a more detailed discussion if only because Coleridge worked on the poem, trying to find some way to bring it to an acceptable conclusion, throughout the period of his greatest poetic productiveness. The poem proceeds from Christabel's failure of self-recognition—the result of her repression of that in herself contradicting an established self-image of innocent virtue. Things are complicated by Christabel's correspondent tendency to avoid such contradiction by denying the distinction between self and world. As a result, she vacillates between treating Geraldine as another person and as an extension of herself. Similarly, the poem vacillates between a moralistic and a psychological treatment of the relationship between the two women. From the psychological viewpoint predominant in Part I, the strength of Christabel's repression determines the demonic aspect of Geraldine's character; and the spell cast by Geraldine reflects the response of a conscious identity based on repression to the unexpected intervention of the unacknowledged self.

When the two women appear before Sir Leoline, Christabel is powerless to deny the statements made by Geraldine. She is even compelled to assume some of her characteristics, becoming the snake in her own garden. Unable to accept the true grounds of her identity with Geraldine, Christabel finds herself in a nightmare in which the power of speech is preempted by the other, unrecognized self and suffers the ordeal of seeing this unacceptable self chosen by her father to represent her. What we see then is the struggle between two parts of the same self to determine which will be repressed.[1]

It may certainly be objected that a purely psychological account ignores the fact that the poem does provide the basis for differentiating between Geraldine and Christabel on moral grounds and encourages us to do so. Geraldine's relationship with Christabel is, however ambivalent, nonetheless predatory. But there is some question as to how we are to understand this moralism in a world in which everyone seems to be acting from motives that are hopelessly obscure or simply irrelevant. Sir Leoline is the representative of social and paternal authority in the poem, but his decision is made in response to his own contingent nostalgia for his friendship with Sir Roland de Vaux. In a world in which such contingen-

---

[1] Edward Strickland has recently published an interesting article in which he argues that "Christabel" involves a confrontation between patent and latent selves (p. 647) and attributes Coleridge's failure to complete the poem to his inability to decide whether Geraldine is a devilish or angelic figure (p. 649). This is important for us because Strickland regards Geraldine as an expression of Coleridge's ambivalent relationship with his own muse (p. 646). We might usefully extend Strickland's argument by observing that the combination of a negative final image of Geraldine with his continued efforts to complete the poem indicate that in this period of his career, Coleridge is being driven by the evidence of his own poetic production to regard poetry in a negative light. It would appear that Coleridge's failures to complete poems are less independent causes than statements in themselves of his poetic condition ("Metamorphoses of the Muse in Romantic Poesis: 'Christabel,'" *English Literary History* 44 [1977]: 641–58).

cies are so pervasive, there is no way to be sure that this moralism is not merely another tactic of repression.

It is precisely the difficulty of containing the psychological questions raised by the poem within the bounds of moral judgment or of identifying any point of view not implicated in the problem of psychological contingency that gives the poem its dark vision and dooms it to incompletion. The attempt to create a narrative romance out of the situation at the poem's center is thwarted by the inaccessibility of a causal center or source of motive. This narrative, the completion of which would signal the accommodation of psychological conflict to moral (and formal) categories, must prove inadequate; for the revelation of psychological contingency blocks all attempts to establish the ontological priority of a narrative, natural, or even personal order.

Coleridge's own final comment on this poem which he was never able to complete, "The Conclusion to Part II," is explicitly concerned with this issue:

> A little child, a limber elf,
> Singing, dancing to itself,[2]
> A fairy thing with red round cheeks,
> That always finds, and never seeks,
> Makes such a vision to the sight
> As fills a father's eyes with light;
> And pleasures flow in so thick and fast
> Upon his heart, that he at last
> Must needs express his love's excess
> With words of unmeant bitterness.

(lines 656–65)

[2] Edward E. Bostetter remarks that the lines "A little child, a limber elf / Singing, dancing to itself" are not to be found in any of the manuscripts of "Christabel." Instead, they appear to be taken from a letter to Southey, dated May 6, 1801, which concerns Coleridge's outbursts of temper at his son, Hartley (*Collected Letters*, ed. E. L. Griggs [Oxford: Oxford University Press, 1956], II, 728). Taken in combination with the discontinuousness of these lines in relation to the body of Part II, Bostetter concludes: "They seem to stand as some kind of obscure comment or cryptogram on the meaning of the poem, perhaps even a clue to the ultimate resolution (*The Romantic Ventriloquists* [Seattle: University of Washington Press, 1963], p. 128).

64 In this startling change of tone and focus, the romance narrative suddenly gives way to domestic reflections on the perversity of our most profound feelings. Although the passage clearly signals Coleridge's decision to give up trying to resolve the psycho-romance of "Christabel" on its own terms, it is nonetheless difficult to know what to make of so radical a discontinuity.

The phenomenon to which Coleridge refers—that of automatically saying the opposite of what we feel under the pressure of intense emotion—is a genuine eruption of psychological contingency into everyday life. Something within the self finds expression in direct contradiction to our conscious understanding of our own feelings and intentions. This unexpected manifestation of an unacknowledged mode of being contradicts any conception of a "natural" order of human response or, rather, exposes the individual to the perpetual possibility of the breakdown of the psychological order which he has conceived for himself and which is an integral part of his identity.

This event bears a close resemblance to statements like "I was promiscuous as a child—promiscuous is not the right word—I was hunting for precocious," which analysts call word-surprises. From the point of view of the analysand, this is simply saying other than what he means. He disclaims responsibility for his utterance by thinking of it as a temporary breakdown in the normal relationship of feeling or thought with language (that is, that utterance is act, giving expression to those thoughts and feelings of which the self is aware). But the analysand's disclaimer, depending as it does on considering utterance as an event, reveals the potential conflict in every utterance between its identity as act and event.

From the analyst's point of view of course, every utterance is an action, and the analysand's disclaimer an evasion. In his book, *Language and Insight*,[3] Roy Schafer remarks about the word-surprise that the analysand says what he does because, for whatever reason, "the surprising word had become the thing to

---

[3] Roy Schafer, *Language and Insight*, Sigmund Freud Memorial Lectures, 1975–76, University College London (New Haven: Yale University Press, 1978), extends and applies the thesis of Schafer's earlier book, *A New Language for Psychoanalysis* (New Haven: Yale University Press, 1976), in which he argued that traditional Freudian terminology imports into the analytic situation an unexamined and inappropriate interpretive model, based on nineteenth-century mechanistic theories of the mind.

say or no longer the thing to refrain from saying." Schafer goes on
to argue:

> Making sense is not limited to the speaker's conscious
> idea of what would make sense or what is consciously in-
> tended. In this respect the speaker clearly does not have
> the last word on what it makes sense to say. My answer
> sets up the word-surprise as a curious text, and it asks how
> this text came to be written. This is to approach the matter
> historically, not causally.[4]

This historical approach to the word-surprise as text seeks

> that which it is necessary to take into account or assume
> in order to understand the action in question. "How else
> could it be?" is what we want to be able to say . . . the
> analyst works backward from the word-surprise to arrive
> at some account of the situation in which saying the
> "wrong" word was the thing to do.[5]

Schafer's word-surprise, like Coleridge's instance of psychological contingency, suggests not only that the self is fragmented but that the fragments do not communicate except indirectly. In the face of direct evidence to the contrary, the analyst's
stance involves a decision to posit a unified intention or identity
behind the diverse, even contradictory, manifestations of behavior.
For the analyst, interpretation is the means by which we contrive
to defend the conviction of identity against the complexity of
behavior by restoring language to the status of act. It is not through
nature or any other inherent order that we mean what we say but
through interpretation. The key factor here is the dialectical relationship between the immediate manifestation of the contingent
and the interpreter's attribution of textuality—the assumption of a
unifying intentional context. Identity then is an act of interpretation

---

[4] Schafer, *Language and Insight*, p. 56.
[5] Ibid., p. 57.

66 which "discovers" its own pretext, thereby confirming its own initiating, even defining, assumption about the ultimate unity of the self.

I do not think it unreasonable to argue that "The Conclusion to Part II" not only discusses the kind of problematic of identity we see in the example of the word-surprise but, in doing so, confronts the poem itself as a word-surprise—an utterance for which the poet is undeniably responsible but which contradicts his understanding of his own intention. As a poem, "Christabel" seeks to naturalize psychic conflict by imposing a progressive, resolvable narrative pattern on a fundamental opposition. But even this is misleading, for the poem's failure questions whether psychic conflict has any form proper to it. The narrative undertaking is defeated by the effects of its necessary allegorical reification of the elements of conflict into two different characters. Eventually, this reification comes to dominate the poem. Christabel and Geraldine are so radically divided, so heavily implicated in the circumstances with which the narrative encumbers them, that there is no way they can be brought together in the context of the poem's psychoromance.

The poem appears to point to the lack of any correspondence between a latent psychological order and any patent, observable order in the world. In attempting to represent the relationship of latent to patent within the limits of a single discourse, Coleridge only demonstrates the self-defeating nature of his attempt to make latency explicit. As its subject, the poem finally takes the asymmetry of observable order and accessible form with internal contents. "The Conclusion to Part II" seeks to restore psychic conflict to latency by providing a new interpretive context for the poem. The domestic anecdote makes possible the abandonment of personification even as it calls attention to the issue of internal contingency. But this new, less threatening origin seems less to exorcise than to minimize the demonic anxieties of the poem. In this regard, "Christabel" provides us with the most immediately and palpably defensive of Coleridge's revisions-by-context.

If we compare "The Conclusion to Part II" with the gloss to "The Rime of the Ancient Mariner" or the preface to "Kubla Khan," we can see that Coleridge eventually confronts each of the Mystery Poems in the manner of the analyst seeking the intentional context, the life history, which will make the word-surprise intelligible as an action. In the Mystery Poems, it is apparent that poetry is in danger of becoming the vehicle of contingency, largely due to Coleridge's inability to find a poetic form—an order—capable of incorporating it. In each of the poems, whatever confirmation of identity is achieved takes place in a retrospective, revisionary addition seeking to achieve for the poem what the life history achieves for the anomalous and self-contradictory word-surprise.

The implications of such a practice are clear: the poem is treated less and less as a self-explanatory, self-sufficient utterance. Indeed, until an intentional context, a satisfactory life history, can be found for it, it is at least potentially a contingent threat to identity. Thus, Coleridge's poetic practice is moving him toward a position that regards uninterpreted poetic utterance as, in some sense, unintelligible. And we can see some of the reasons for Coleridge's concern with the problem of the text, especially with differentiating the individual text, as a possibly anomalous manifestation, from textuality, as the pretext and goal of interpretation— the order within which psychological contingency can be contained and identity assured.

In "The Rime of the Ancient Mariner," the gloss represents an attempt to encompass the events of the poem within some rational order. So pervasive are the gloss's impositions that many of the things which we regard as being said in the poem, or at least apparent in its form, are actually asserted or assumed only in the gloss. It is the gloss that jumps to the conclusion that there is some kind of causal relationship between the appearance of the albatross and the release of the ice-bound ship. While the poem tersely states "With my cross-bow / I shot the Albatross" (lines 81–2), the gloss imposes on this act its own framework of judgment and value: "The ancient Mariner inhospitably killeth the pious bird of good omen."

As subsequent events prove, this moralistic framework, based on a simple economy of things, clearly relating cause and effect, act and punishment, on the basis of coincidence, is grossly inadequate to enclose the psychological contingency revealed in the mariner's act—an act frightening in its irreducibility to any explanation, an act which must be presented as unmotivated because its motivation is somewhere in a self that we do not recognize

68 or acknowledge.[6] What the poem suggests, and the obvious inadequacy of the gloss seems to confirm, is the inaccessibility of will to rationalization.

The gloss's interest in accommodating poetic events to moral categories and its particular dependence on coincidence points to its fundamentally allegorical understanding of the poem as a text. As we have remarked before, Coleridge's objection to allegory has to do with the arbitrariness with which it relates a figurative order of meaning with literal objects or events. Within an allegorical poem, for example, meaning is perceived through a coincidence of the literal and the figurative which is recognized to be intentional. The gloss to "The Rime of the Ancient Mariner" brings to the poem an insistence on seeing signs in literal events. But in this case, the gloss lacks the understanding of the interpretive pretext or life history of the poem which normally sustains allegory. The inadequacy of the gloss's attempts at allegorization to enclose the action of the poem or to disclose the order conditioning the apparent contingency governing the world in which the mariner finds himself reveals that coincidence is not a sufficient ground of meaning. What the gloss-poem relationship points to is the inability of allegory to function as an interpretive (as opposed to expressive) mode when the intentional context of the object of interpretation is not already clearly defined. Thus, we can say that the gloss fails to define the terms upon which this poem is a unified text because allegory and perhaps even figuration are themselves insufficient definitions of the poetic text.

The gloss, like "The Conclusion to Part II," represents Coleridge's self-conscious and retrospective comment on the life history of the poem. By its own failure, the gloss calls attention to the failure within the poem of figuration to impose some order on psychological contingency. Instead of being tamed and contained within a figurative order, the contingency revealed in the shooting of the albatross reaches out and takes over the instruments of figuration so that the sensible world is manipulated from sources

[6] James D. Boulger comments on the failures within the poem of "syllogistic logic" in a world of effects whose causes are unknown in "Christian Skepticism in 'The Rime of the Ancient Mariner,'" in *From Sensibility to Romanticism: Essays Presented to Frederick A. Pottle*, ed. Frederick W. Hilles and Harold Bloom (Oxford: Oxford University Press, 1965), pp. 445–46.

within the self invisible to the amazed and terrified mariner. The
inaccessibility of will (or an ultimate source of motive) to rationalization is projected as a demonized world or blind allegory.
The poem does not subdue or reconcile itself to psychological contingency so much as it manages to extricate itself from its most
extreme consequences.

However, the mariner does not escape unscarred from
his sojourn in the world made self. His delivery from the nightmare world does not enable him to appropriate his experience
either to his own identity or to his conception of the identity
of the natural world. The only alternative to appropriation is the
repression of this demonic self, a repression which exposes the
mariner to periodic returns:

> Since then at an uncertain hour,
> That agony returns:
> And till my ghastly tale is told,
> This heart within me burns.
>
> I pass, like night, from land to land;
> I have strange powers of speech;
> That moment that his face I see,
> I know the man that must hear me:
> To him my tale I teach.

> (lines 582–90)

The mariner is exiled from a revelation central to his life by his
inability to revise as well as repeat; he is doomed to an endless
search for his own prophetic reader.

The conditions making possible the mariner's very limited salvation are defined in this passage in which he first feels
the grip of the nightmare world loosening:

> The moving Moon went up the sky,
> And no where did abide:

70

> Softly she was going up,
> And a star or two beside—
>
> Her beams bemocked the sultry main,
> Like April hoar-frost spread;
> But where the ship's huge shadow lay,
> The charmed water burnt alway
> A still and awful red.
>
> (lines 263–71)

Then the mariner's attention shifts to the sea snakes leaving wakes of phosphorescent fire behind them as they swarm around the ship:

> Oh happy living things! no tongue
> Their beauty might declare:
> A spring of love gushed from my heart,
> And I blessed them unaware:
> Sure my kind saint took pity on me,
> And I blest them unaware.
>
> (lines 282–87)

Suddenly the mariner is able to confront the snakes, not as projections of his own self-loathing but as something genuinely other and beautiful in their own right. His spontaneous blessing is another Coleridgean act of bestowal—an evidence of the mariner's release from a relentless logic of self-enclosure which distorts in its own image, by the force of the self's demand on the world, every attempt to reach out and contact the "other."

But where does this ability come from? Is it simply that the self cannot sustain the pressure of its own demand and thus withdraws from the external world in response to some secret economy of its own? If so, the mariner's release is not an escape from the grip of psychological contingency; it is merely the revelation of another aspect of that contingency. It is certainly not much reassurance of the ultimate control of conscious identity over the self. The pretext for this change is identified as the moon in the longest and most circumstantial of the glosses on the poem:

> In his loneliness and fixedness he yearneth towards the journeying Moon, and the stars that still sojourn, yet still move onward; and every where the blue sky belongs to them, and is their appointed rest, and their native country and their own natural homes, which they enter unannounced, as lords that are certainly expected and yet there is a silent joy at their arrival.

The gloss resists the contingency of the mariner's release by identifying the appearance of the moon as its pretext and by inventing an elaborately circumstantial interpretation of the moon's significance which is apparently aimed at making one point: the moon does not fit into whatever figurative structure which the unrecognized part of the mariner's self, his unacknowledged intention, is projecting onto the external world. Because the moon and stars—an unpolluted otherness—successfully resist incorporation into whatever "text" the contingent self is seeking to impose, the mariner is suddenly released from his "fixedness."

The oft-remarked suggestion of allegory in forming the poem, coupled with the absence of any achieved allegorical structure, points in the direction of a fundamental relationship between the arbitrariness of allegorical figuration and the unexpectedness of self-experience. In the absence of a clearly defined external perspective, like that provided by the moon, allegory can become completely subsumed into a self only imperfectly understood. "The Rime of the Ancient Mariner" seems to be moving toward a recognition that we must either define in some form outside the self the intentional context relating meanings and objects or be engulfed by our own psychological contingencies. It is also made pretty clear that allegory, a concept of figuration tied to the view that poetry is expressive in nature and arbitrary in the relationships it assigns between literal signs and subjective signifieds, can never be an adequate instrument for seeking out the truth of our relationship to the world, for in the absence of a clearly defined intentional context, it betrays us to the contingency of our own selves. The impli-

72  cation of this is, in turn, that literature, insofar as it is defined allegorically, promotes our isolation from rather than integration with the world around.

What the gloss on the moon implies is that natural objects are only so malleable in regard to the meanings we wish to impose on them. This is not necessarily to argue that an object like the moon has a particular meaning as an attribute of its objective identity. Instead, it can be argued that objects accumulate meaning because of the uses to which we put them. Thus, the moon can be associated with a great number of meanings, but there are also some meanings whose association with the moon will be absurd. This moves us toward a symbolic conception of the nature of figuration (and the temptation is strong to say simply that the demonic allegory is interrupted by the inadvertent recognition of a genuine symbol) but still leaves unanswered the question: what is the instrument by which meaning adheres to objects? What is its status and how can it be defined? These are questions for which "The Rime of the Ancient Mariner" presents no answer, and that is why the mariner is temporarily extricated but not saved from his nightmare world.

Up to this point, I have not had much to say about one of the most obvious features of the Mystery Poems: their supernaturalism. In "The Rime of the Ancient Mariner," the supernatural plays a tremendous role because its resistance to allegorization argues the inadequacy of the concept of natural order to represent either the order of the self or the order of the text. The poem's deployment of supernatural objects and events to represent the mariner's contingent subjectivity indicates that there is a whole range of human thoughts and feelings which, because of the urgency of their demand or the strength with which they have been repressed, cannot find adequate signification within the realm of the natural order. The contingency of these mental contents with relation to the conscious self, the established identity, also makes them contingent in relation to any order which is part of the knowledge possessed by the identity of the self and correspondent with it.

Natural signifiers function within a conception of natural order—they have already been appropriated to a conception of the identity of nature corresponding in some way to the identity of the self. This means that the signifiers of a psychological contingency must be unnatural—not only outside any established order of nature, but themselves disordered. The supernatural is not an extension of nature, not above or below it; it is supernatural precisely because it stands in a radically indeterminate relation to nature. The indeterminacy of this relationship is a consequence of the radically indeterminate relationship between psychological contingency and identity.

If we turn back to the mariner, we can see that his refusal to accept or to acknowledge his contingent self creates, by the very strength of its repression, contingency as the principle of misrule governing the world around. But there is also a suggestion in the poem that the revelation of an internal contingency results from the self's excessive demand on the external world—a demand for an ever more precise correspondence between the order of nature and the order of the self. Normally, the self confines itself to those thoughts, feelings, and actions which can be signified and thus contained within some concept of the natural order, the identity of nature. In this sense, what we call nature becomes the instrument of repression in defense of the identity of the self. But the identity of the self is in constant danger of upsetting its own order and what it regards as the natural order by the excess of its demand. This isolation and guilt that plagues the mariner represents a failure of accommodation in which the inability to accept the "otherness" of the external world without anxiety and aggression corresponds to an inability to accept the fundamental strangeness of self to itself.

The role of the psychologically contingent in disrupting not only the order of the self but the order of the other as well reveals just how dangerous a tool allegorical figuration is and points to the need for a better definition of the figurative order in its relationship to the orders of nature, the self, and the text. There is the implication that through figuration, the poet himself becomes the limit of order. The problem with this is the inadequacy of the subjective categories which the poet imposes on his psychological being. It is the demonstrated inadequacy of subjective categories, of self-definition, which constitutes the Mystery Poems' most devastating critique

74 of the projective mode of the Conversation Poems, in which order itself is dependent upon conscious identity's power to accommodate self-experience to natural signifiers.

It remains to be said with regard to projection that "The Rime of the Ancient Mariner" also suggests that what lies behind an ordered nature, thoroughly conditioned by established displacements like the Philomel story of "The Nightingale," is not unmediated nature but a deeper level of projection, revealing to the self thoughts and feelings it did not know it had—powerfully repressed materials which the self is reluctant to accept as its own. This implies that an excessive dependence upon the external world to signify and thus define the world within—which is also a dependence upon the sufficiency of figuration to define relationships between subjective and objective categories of being—can lead to the total rejection of the external world in an attempt to disclaim responsibility for unsuspected and unacceptable aspects of the self.

The contextual revisions of "Christabel" and "The Rime of the Ancient Mariner" discussed earlier make their points largely by their inadequacy as responses to the unexpected revelations of the poems. By contrast, the preface to "Kubla Khan" offers a powerful voice, pitting its own interpretive fiction against the vision of the poem. The preface exploits assumptions about the greater proximity of prose to the literal in order to appropriate to itself the powers of prophetic expression normally included among the pretensions of poetry. In an earlier chapter, we clarified the relationship between the preface and some of the philosophical concerns contemporary with it; earlier in this chapter, we discussed the ways in which contextual revision selects and emphasizes certain threatening implications of Coleridge's own poetic practice. Now, in light of what we have learned, it is time to return to "Kubla Khan" in order to examine more closely Coleridge's most radical questionings of the nature of poetic privilege.

To begin with Coleridge's (first) beginning, there is Kubla's creating word. Or, more precisely, the poem begins in the indeterminate aftermath and goes on to explore the fate of vision and the visionary banished from the place of utterance, from the original Word. What the poem offers is not the Word but a description of the Word—"decree." And this description cannot be distinguished from the pleasure dome, which is our only clue to the content of the Word. Thus, the oft-remarked perfection of Kubla's will, creating by decree, is evidence of the impossibility of distinguishing the Word from the objective space into which it has been dispersed. Kubla's created order of dome and garden stands between us and the Word, demanding either that we interpret them as a text or accept a permanent exile.

Efforts to get back to an original utterance are frustrated by the fact that in becoming, the Word has already accepted the limitations of its "creator" as well as of its embodied form. The inability of even the most perfected will to speak an order into existence is suggested by Kubla's attempt to measure out "twice five miles of fertile ground" on the very borders of a realm "measureless to man." So close to the "sunless sea" where he is necessarily blind, Kubla must shut his eyes to the limits of sight and even insight. Trying to begin with the beginning, the poem becomes a progressive revelation of the depths of repression involved in trying to get around, above, or behind the "mere" embodiment, the "mere" description of the Word.

The return to the original scene of utterance, which is also an attempt to limit the dispersion of the Word by decree, requires no less than the repression of the world and exposes the individual to the perpetual threat of the return of the repressed—"ancestral voices prophesying war." The price of returning to the Word of pure prophecy is to turn everything else into a prophecy of destruction.

The more tightly we cling to the origin, the more limited we are by our own creations. Refusing to accept the loss of the Word, Kubla's unrestrained imaginative desire makes him the prisoner of his own decree, of the simultaneity of utterance and embodiment. Kubla's effort to transcend the mediate and to evade belatedness through an act of will makes of him an image of man's willful ignorance of his own condition, and a compelling poetic self-image.

The limitations of Kubla's created order as a description (signified? figure?) of the Word are immediately apparent. His walls and towers merely assert the symmetry of inside/outside with natural order/disorder. The effort necessary to thrust back or out or down something which nevertheless insists on remaining close at hand charges the chasm with demonic attributes: "A savage

76 place! as holy and enchanted / As e'er beneath a waning moon was haunted / By woman wailing for her demon lover" (lines 14–16). Less interesting as a description than as a revelation of repression, these lines suggest that the spectre haunting the chasm is the self's knowledge of the self-imposed isolation resulting from the limitation of consciousness by will or desire. If the apprehension of this nature outside created order results in this unexpected revelation—this vision of nature haunted by the self grieving for an image of itself—then perhaps our difficulty is not so much in transcending the descriptive as in avoiding such unwelcome and unexpected revelations.

In the chasm, the plights of Kubla and the poet are brought closer together by the challenge of describing a scene that is more than "merely" natural—at once of nature and outside normative ideas of the natural. In this space between conception and event is revealed the essentially figurative nature of all description in a world ruled by the interplay of will and repression. Description unexpectedly betrays the ambiguity of figuration as an instrument of creative will and conscious intent on the one hand, and as a discipline externalizing and objectifying that will in unexpected, even shocking ways on the other.

This relationship between figuration and repression is elaborated when the comparison with "chaffy grain beneath the thresher's flail" moves beyond the descriptive into the realm of the apocalyptic. Striving to keep up with the sublime violence of the scene, description gains such momentum that it breaks simultaneously out of the realm of mimesis and out of the realm of the natural. It issues not into a realm above or below or behind nature, but into another poem, Jeremiah (23:28, on distinguishing true from false prophecy). Driving language along the road of the natural sublime, we arrive not at the Word but at the text or mediate form of another prophecy.

Conceived as originating prophecy then, the poem leads back to the knowledge that the prophecy has already been uttered elsewhere and that as prophecy, the poem is extraneous. Conceived prophetically or not, what this and every other poem represses is the awareness that the common language of figuration makes it difficult to keep other texts at a distance, to maintain the distinction between description and allusion. Thus, the poem approaches the recognition that poetry and the Word are antithetical. If when the Word was given to Adam, everything worth writing was given with it, then the poet's belated writings are at best a sign of his distance from the Word and a confirmation of another's prophecy.

The explicit connection made between fountain and caves (lines 21–28) invites us to complete an intimated allegory of nature by imagining a similar connection beneath the earth's surface. Reading the visible as an allegory of the invisible, we could then envision nature as an order enfolding initiation and closure within the assurance of an eternal return. Which is to say that we would be able to see nature as the reply confirming the presence of the Word. But whatever allegorical order, if any, encloses the fountain and the caves, it manifests itself beyond sight. The alternative is, of course, insight, which presents its own difficulties. As we have seen, the attempt to will insight through a figurative repression of the literal scene/seen not only exposes the poet to a return of the repressed but results in displacement rather than transcendence. The allegorization of nature eventually confirms the absence of the Word, presenting the poet with the "revelation" that all orders created/perceived are horizontal and simultaneous, presenting themselves to each other as principles of contingency, and are not vertical and hierarchical, proceeding from immanent to transcendent.

Ironically, the source of the poet's anxiety is his sensation that in reaching for the originating Word, he is losing his grasp on the literality of his own words. Hence, the true analogue of the poet's search for the internal source of his own discourse is the increasing indistinctness of nature as figurative displacement progresses under the pressure of the will to allegory. Vision, as word and idea, is a perfect embodiment of this loss. The word is itself a figure for a relationship between sight and insight—a relationship in which each becomes an allegory of the other. The allegorical nature of the sight/insight relationship becomes, in its turn, a sign of the mutual exclusivity of sight and insight at the level of the literal.

Coleridge's movement toward the visionary reappropriation of the Word becomes a kind of antiprophecy, revealing the incompatibility of sight/insight, the Word and words. Vision as a poetic self-image brings the poet to see himself trapped within an

78    allegory whose intentional context is the mystery at the heart of the
Word. Thus, it is the Word itself which becomes the Covering
Cherub preventing the poet from confirming the literality of con-
sciousness in the literality of his own words.

In the context of such disturbing implications, the poem
approaches the kind of resolution associated with the Conversation
Poems:

> The shadow of the dome of pleasure
> Floated midway on the waves;
> Where was heard the mingled measure
> From the fountain and the caves.
> It was a miracle of rare device.
> A sunny pleasure-dome with caves of ice!

> (lines 31–36)

As a resolution, these lines are hardly more than a juxtaposition of
terms. Within the narrow space of six lines, cave-dome, dome-
wave, and sun-ice are held in solution. But we are no longer in a
position to accept this as a triumph of reconciliation rather than a
failure of distinction. At issue here is the power of the poetic word,
as an extension of poetic will, to "decree" a fusion of opposing
terms. Echoing and answering Kubla's earlier decree, this visionary resolution also echoes the belatedness of Kubla's towers
and walls.

The poem's movement toward vision is thwarted here by
the obtrusive poetic paradox of willing a vision. Thus, these lines
indicate the absence of the Word in all its mysterious unifying
force and suggest an antithesis of poetry and vision, of poetry and
the Word. Nor does this visionary language succeed in naming
(rather than figuring) itself. The self-comprehending image of
reflection reveals that there is another Word behind the one uttered
here and, furthermore, that that word is condemnatory:

> The other are but empty echoes which the fancy arbitrarily
> associates with apparitions of matter, less beautiful, but

not less shadowy than the sloping orchard or hill-side 79
pasture-field seen in the transparent lake below.

(*SM*, 30–31)

"The other" are of course allegories, suggesting that within the
context of poetry, allegory and vision share the same limitations
and that both point to the absence of the Word.

Coleridge's vision fails quite literally to be the last (final)
word, and that failure is evidenced in the abrupt fall out of vision
indicated by the new distance of:

> A damsel with a dulcimer
> In a vision once I saw:
> It was an Abysinnian maid,
> And on her dulcimer she played
> Singing of Mount Abora.

(lines 37–41)

Our attention is first arrested by the opacity of this new retrospective vision. Since it is all but contextless, there is no way to establish
its meaning. This circumstance invites us to consider the possibility
that there is no way for the visionary to bring his vision back into
the realm of the literal. Here vision is not presented as a distinct
object, available to interpretation. Instead, it includes the visionary
within itself, and for the duration of the vision, he shares its discontinuity. When he steps out of the vision (or, rather, when it
passes him by), it assumes an opaque aspect. To cling to the lost
vision, to continue to assert its centrality, is to make the self a prisoner of a self-created mystery.

The poem's final image of inspired but exclusive poetic
frenzy refers us to the poet as isolated and self-involved victim of
his own mystification (if he insists that poetry is vision) and to the
poet's fear that if he regards poetry as a craft or extension of will,
he will be left with those baffled spectators—a looker-on forever
excluded from the heart of things.

80     This last section of the poem clearly articulates the dilemma of the poet pursuing a visionary insight into a transcendent ontology, all the while aware that he is willing the acts of figuration by which that vision comes into being. "Kubla Khan" forces on its poet the recognition that insofar as he is a poet, vision is only a figure. Within the bounds of poetry there is no escape from the "merely" figurative; and as long as the poet links the identity of the self to the identity of the Word, he remains trapped in an indeterminate relationship of the willed and the true.

In the second (and "real") beginning there is Purchas' *Pilgrimage*—a book made significant by the fact that it was one of Milton's sources. Coleridge's assertion that Purchas is the origin (not source) of the poem corresponds to an effort within the poem to obliterate evidence of its sources. In his article, "Coleridge and the Ancestral Voices," Brisman notes Coleridge's revision of the Miltonic echo "Amara" to "Abora" and speculates that "Abora" may refer to the aboriginal word.[7] In Brisman's view, Coleridge's attempt to get behind Milton to Purchas, and then behind Purchas to a word so aboriginal that it is now meaningless, is a way of achieving priority by making his poem the context in which that lost word can once again be spoken meaningfully.

Brisman's larger argument about "Kubla Khan," focusing on the intrusion of the man from Porlock, is an important one and deserves detailed treatment here. Brisman begins with some of Coleridge's own attacks on source hunting as a critical enterprise. For Coleridge, this kind of reading-back reflects an impulse to naturalize genius, conceiving it as an outgrowth rather than as a new dispensation. The tyranny of texts over the originality of the mind is linked to the notion that when the alphabet was given to Adam, everything worth writing was given with it. In this context, "Kubla Khan" can be seen as a prophetic attempt to circumvent the text as source and to take the path back to the liberating, Adamic Word —the Word ensuring the priority of genius in all times and places.

But Coleridge's poetic rebellion against a false belatedness is interrupted by the man from Porlock. This primal scene, says Brisman, represses Coleridge's awareness that he is his own interruptor, externalizing what is really an internal division. Por-

---

[7] Leslie Brisman, *Romantic Origins* (Ithaca: Cornell University Press, 1978), pp. 21–33.

lock represents the conflict, reconstructed in Coleridge's verse, between the person and the poet. As the spectre of his natural self, Porlock is "unwilling to recognize his subordinate status of interpreter to a more original text." Thus, Porlock "knows and wrestles with his secondariness, making strange alliances through which he can 're-originate' in a poem (as Milton's serpent does entering Eden) and thus penetrate the wish-fulfillment character of lyric vision."[8]

Two points must be noted before we begin to construct an alternative reading. First, there is nothing in Coleridge's remarks on source hunting that *compels* the kind of implicit judgment that Brisman makes against Porlock on behalf of Coleridge the poet. Second, the remarks that I have already made on the poem proper indicate that it is at least possible to read it in a way that contradicts such a judgment. We can find common ground between Brisman's reading and the remarks that I have already offered by observing that Coleridge moves between the self-images of Kubla and Porlock. For Brisman, Kubla represents genius and Porlock natural man. We can lift some of the burden of Brisman's implicit judgment by further observing that the Kubla self-image is poetic and serves as a vehicle for prophetic or visionary desire; the Porlock self-image is expressed in prose which serves as the vehicle of limitation.

Brisman's understanding of Porlock makes of the preface an interruption of a lyric movement toward the fulfillment of poetic desire. But it should be noted that the repression of internal conflict as "interruption" is presented in the context of the preface—a context which makes of the involuntary repression a conscious choice. For, paradoxically, nothing is so representative of choice, consciously and retrospectively made, as a preface. The Porlockian interruption can also be seen then as a way of representing the poet's recognition that such limitation is necessary if the lyric movement toward the fulfillment of desire is not to result in disastrous disillusionment. As I have suggested, the unbalanced pursuit of the Kubla self-image may result in the negative revelation of the poet's permanent exile from the Adamic Word.

The preface also suggests that prior to the problem of the

[8] Ibid., pp. 32, 33.

82 originating Word is the problem of Coleridge's relation to his own creating word. Coleridge's movement away from the Miltonic "Amara" to "Abora" can also be understood as an indication of Coleridge's recognition that the exile from his own word (or, rather, from the conception of his poetry as a visionary reflection of the creating Word) is the price of avoiding the fate of the frenzied and isolated visionary poet. The preface finally represses not the loss of the poem as creating word but the renunciation which is its real content. In this way, Coleridge maintains a delicate ambiguity about the visionary lyric, endorsing the value of lyric aspiration while rejecting the fate of the visionary poet.

Returning once again to Coleridge's Amara-Abora revision, we can see how the preface displaces away from source as a naturalistic conception of poetry toward origin—a concept elevating the beginning chosen as most desirable over that imposed in the order of things. The account of the prose preface separates the original lines in Purchas from the poem with an unknown space in which genius operates unimpaired. Seen in this way, the preface as Porlockian interruption answers to lyric desire more effectively than the poem itself, even as it rejects the sufficiency of vision or lyric alone to define poetic or intellectual identity.

Brisman's conception of the poem as a search for the ab-original word seems to me related to E. S. Shaffer's recent argument that "Kubla Khan" is the densely impacted fragment of Coleridge's projected epic *The Fall of Jerusalem*.[9] For Coleridge, the Jews' awareness of themselves as a nation originated in the prophetic revelation of Old Testament law. Their loss of temporal power and subsequent diaspora was the result of their failure to understand that no word, however prophetic, is literal in relation to the Word—that what was received in the form of an injunction to obey and a promise of temporal reward was not so much a prophecy as a preface to a future prophetic revelation of an eternal or nontemporal reward. Similarly, Kubla's decree, as close to the literal word as it is, is nonetheless belated in relation to the negating literality of the caverns "measureless to man" and "sunless sea."

The largely indeterminate relationship between preface

[9] E. S. Shaffer, *"Kubla Khan" and The Fall of Jerusalem* (Cambridge: Cambridge University Press, 1975), pp. 18–19.

and poem, emphasizing that they are equally mediate in relation to the word (that is, that poetry is not privileged by greater proximity to origins) reflects Coleridge's awareness that for him there is no literal word, only prefaces to a prophecy coming into being. The error of the Jews was in believing that the temporal "word" of their kingdom was an answer to and fulfillment of the Word—that they were speaking the same language, and that prophecy could be fulfilled and hence read aright at any moment but the last. Similarly, the end of "Kubla Khan" suggests that the lyric desire of the visionary poet for the aboriginal word is fulfilled only as the poet himself disappears into his vision.

Unless one is God, historical events (or literary acts) are not fulfillments of prophecy so much as additions confirming or denying existing understandings. Prophecy comes into being in history; history is not merely the means by which prophecy is fulfilled. The relationship between "Kubla Khan" and its preface is the finite repetition of the intersection of prophecy and history in the Bible. The preface to "Kubla Khan" parodies the way in which the Bible is the subsequent prophetic interpretation that revises and assumes priority: it prophesies a failure of the poem, which is really a "decree."

The preface bases its claim to priority on its revelation that the poem has a history that negates rather than confirms it. Pitting historical revelation against poetic prophecy, Coleridge suggests that the revelation of the Word in history (in the Bible) is a sign of its absence as Word—of its diaspora into language. The absence of the literal word suggests the impossibility of *poetic* vision. Instead, the poem is another event through which the prophecy that the poet is blindly acting out comes into being.

In this context, "Kubla Khan" may be seen as an elaborate ritual of renunciation: it refuses to assert its self-fulfillment (it is a fragment); it asserts its failure as a vision; it is revised in order to avoid claiming to complete or fulfill Milton; it eventually denies even that it is a poem. Yet none of these renunciations, any more than the poem's complementary, assertive countermovement, is sufficient to recover the aboriginal word. Rather, they suggest that even if we could recover it, it would now be meaningless.

The question of the Bible, pursued in *The Statesman's Manual*, in *Biographia* XVII, in the *Friend*, in *Aids to Reflection*, and in *Confessions of an Inquiring Spirit*, is not only central to the preface-poem relationship in "Kubla Khan"; it is central to understanding that poem's importance for the rest of the canon. It is the Bible as text that stands between the inaccessible unity of the divine Word and the hopeless fragmentation of natural language. The indeterminacy of the preface-poem relationship reflects an awareness that both are equally mediate and that their proper paradigm should be the biblical model of the text, not the originating Word.

Having pushed this line of investigation onto grounds more directly addressed elsewhere in Coleridge's work, let us return to consider the preface as a retrospective critique of Coleridge's relationship with his own poems. At the center of the preface is the startling claim:

> The author continued for about three hours in a profound sleep, at least of the external senses, during which time he has the most vivid confidence, that he could not have composed less than from two to three-hundred lines; if that can be called composition in which all the images rose up before him as *things*, with the parallel production of the correspondent expressions, without any sensation or consciousness of effort. On awaking he appeared to himself to have a distinct recollection of the whole, and taking his pen, ink, and paper instantly and eagerly wrote down the lines that are here preserved.

By calling the poem "A Vision in a Dream" and by presenting it as a "psychological curiosity," Coleridge himself raises the question of whether an utterance that circumvents the creative will can be called a poem at all. But the primary proposition being tested here is that the suspension of the will brings us closer to the truth, that utterance unaffected by will is less figurative and more literal and therefore closer to a vision or prophecy of the Word.

The preface must also be seen as an exploration of the poet's exile from the Word in its relation to the psychologically contingent—the element of self-revelation giving the poem its demonic quality in the eyes of Coleridge the prefator. What the poet faces in the preface is the massive contradiction of his conscious identity as poet—a revelation of a self he neither knows nor controls. It is precisely the discontinuity between poetic identity and discontinuous visionary utterance that prevents the poem from assuming the literality of vision or prophecy. It is in the nature of the situation that these lines be seen as *representing* this contingent self, rather than as a literal utterance. The implication is that although he can, perhaps must, attribute prophetic qualities to others, he cannot be a prophet to himself and a poet too. He is most powerful not in the role of prophetic voice but in that of prophetic reader—a role entailing his alienation from his own externalized discourse.

In this account, the man from Porlock is, as a figure or representation, overdetermined. His interruption represents identity's defense against its own contingency, and against the defining power of utterance as a revelation of that contingency. And we cannot ignore the possibility—supported by the fact that the poet "only appeared to himself to have a distinct recollection of the whole"—that the poet's conviction was simply wrong and that the Porlockian interruption is a defense against the inaccessibility of his own words' literality. We must, in any case, recognize the inevitability of such an intrusion. Sooner or later the prophetic or visionary speaker must come down from the mountain and return to the world of men, suffering the consequent loss of the sensation or conviction of his visionary state. Thus, we can also see the intrusion as a recognition that vision is not a thing to be examined so much as a subjectivity momentarily shared by prophet and prophecy. The prophetic nature of an utterance is not inherent; it must be constructed in an act of reading rather than speaking. No prophecy but the first is other than interpretive.

The preface itself ends with such an instance of prophetic revision directed at one of Coleridge's own poems: "The Picture; or, the Lover's Resolution" (1802). According to the preface, when Coleridge returned to his room after being interrupted, he

found, to his no small surprise and mortification, that although he still retained some vague and dim recollection of the general purport of his vision, yet, with the exception of some eight or ten scattered lines and images, all the rest had passed away like the images on the surface of a stream into which a stone has been cast, but, alas! without the after restoration of the latter!

The permanent loss of the vision is inseparable from the loss of a conception of the relationship between poet and poem. No longer can he count on encountering his own gaze reflected in his poems. This image of reflection both repeats and rejects the central image of reconciliation offered in the poem itself: that of the dome reflected in the river. In the poem, this static image of resolution proves only an accident of juxtaposition, created and then obliterated in the movement of the poem's language. Like the Jews' Jerusalem—a prophetic culmination denied by the continuous flow of history—the image is a culmination contradicted by the refusal of discourse and consciousness alike to accept its limitations.

The lines from "The Picture" quoted by Coleridge describe the poet-lover contemplating the image of a beautiful woman amidst the reflections of trees, flowers, and sky. A flower falls into the water (we are told that it is dropped into the pool by the woman), and the image dissolves. When the water settles, the woman is gone and the poet turns to pursue the reality or literality of his vision. It is never made clear that there was a real woman, that she was not the naiad to which she is compared. In "The Picture," reflection indicates the uncertain relationship between nature and desire. In "Kubla Khan," it indicates the uncertain relationship between desire—especially desire for self-image or confirmation—and poetry. The permanent loss of the reflection and the irreversible disturbance of the calm surface of the poem represent the transmutation of the intense, mutual gaze of the self and lyric poetry into a series of displaced problematics of uncertain relation: inclusion-exclusion, order-contingency, poetic-natural, figurative-literal, conscious-unconscious, will-vision.

In their readings, both Brisman and Shaffer seek to document and emphasize the poem as lyric compression, seeking the dense center or origin—an impacting. But the preface, with its image of an image of reflection dissolving into ripples, signals the triumph of a centrifugal countermovement, best interpreted in terms of a figure unavailable to Coleridge. In "Kubla Khan," the lyric as an impacting of vision and poetry, limitation and desire, reaches its critical mass and explodes outward into the fragmented problematics with which Coleridge struggles for the rest of his career to recreate into some semblance of an order capable of reconciling the willed (or desired) and the true.

In their different ways, poem and preface ultimately designate the loss or absence of the Word. This loss simultaneously defines their closest similarity and greatest difference: in the poem, the loss is acknowledged, but not as a necessary consequence of the conditions of being; in the preface, the loss or exile from the Word is confronted as inherent in the nature of things. In any case, it is the absence, rather than a presence, that guarantees the relationship between prose preface and poem. In dealing with the intimate relationship between the absence of the Word and the fullness of the text, nothing separates a modern critic like Paul de Man from Coleridge more clearly than de Man's conclusion that this absence at the center of writing, the impossibility of the Word ever being present, defines the ontology central to reading and writing alike.[10] Coleridge draws an equally valid conclusion that this point of absence, equally central to "Kubla Khan" as an act of writing and as an instance of (self)reading, where sight and insight are one, is the Bible. Such a conclusion is at once immanent in the language of the poem (the poem itself reveals the absence at its center, corresponding to the unique qualities of the biblical text); and it moves us beyond the "poetic" into the realm of biblical revelation. The paradigm for this peculiar combination of immanence and transcendence resides in the Bible's unique identity as both a book and not a book, and in the correspondent doubleness of history and revelation.

In the preface to "Kubla Khan," Coleridge redefines his poem, as he did with "Christabel" and "The Rime of the Ancient Mariner," in terms of the word-surprise. He claims in this case, however, that the contingent asserted itself to the extent of appropriating to itself all the creative instruments of the conscious self. What the preface intimates is that in the absence of some "order"

10 Paul de Man, *Blindness and Insight* (Oxford: Oxford University Press, 1971), pp. 17–19.

88 with a clearly defined relationship to the contingent, a poem can be "true" only insofar as it is not a poem.

Coleridge is brought to this point, I think, by his difficulty in conceiving of any accurate way to represent his own paradoxical modes of poetic behavior, except in terms of two personified selves. The internalization and psychologizing of an inherently dichotomous subject-object terminology threatens to make the man the prisoner of his self-representation, committing him irrevocably to mutually uncomprehending self-images.[11] One of the most interesting and suggestive things that this situation emphasizes about Coleridge is the degree to which his personal difficulties lend themselves to formulation in religious, philosophical, or literary terms.

Among the purposes of this discussion has been the explanation of Coleridge's virtual abandonment of poetry. In a sense, the Mystery Poems are an explanation in themselves, for they indicate not only the degree to which Coleridge is alienated from his own poetic practice but also his conviction that he does not understand his own poetry. This is important because it is Coleridge's basic ability to comprehend his personal alienation and the accompanying anxiety as a failure of understanding—something to be remedied by an improved comprehension—that determines the subsequent course of his career.

Given the fact of alienation, Coleridge can either regard it as a fundamental failure of the person, which would be to accept his inability to control his own contingent self, or he can regard it as a failure of the persona or self-representation, at least theoretically remediable by accessible intellectual means. Conceiving of his personal difficulties as a failure in his understanding of his own intellectual-artificing persona, Coleridge is able to subdue partially and give objective definition to the complexities of his own nature by subsuming them into an attempt to correct his failure to understand properly the nature of the poetic text—a failure to

---

[11] Schafer's development of his concept of an "action language" for psychoanalysis involves an extended critique of the concept of motivation, especially in connection with a representation of conflict based on two distinct entities, each designated "self." Significantly, Schafer emphasizes the concept of the text, applied to the materials of analysis, as a means of avoiding this representative scheme and the model of the self which it implies (*Language and Insight*, pp. 67–103).

understand the proper context of figurative acts, including acts of self-representation. Coleridge's pursuit of this context over the remainder of his career in *The Statesman's Manual*, in the "Method" essays, in Volume II of *Biographia*, in *Aids to Reflection* and *Confessions of an Inquiring Spirit* is informed by the insight that any conflict or problem that is manifested in a text—that is susceptible of textual representation—refers back to the preconditions of textuality itself. This insight leads Coleridge to the Bible and ultimately to a vision of writing as the means by which men and events are appropriated, generation by generation, to the continuity of biblical history.

# 4

## BIBLICAL HISTORY
## AND THE AUTHOR'S SHARE:

*The Statesman's Manual*

The original title of *The Statesman's Manual—The Bible the Best Guide to Political Skill and Foresight*—suggests that at the broadest level of conception, the book is concerned with the evasive literality of belief and especially with the difficulties of discovering (or creating) that literality in the shape of the state and the quality of its leadership. For Coleridge, the complex immanence of belief in society is prefigured in the immanence of the Word in the words of the Bible. *The Statesman's Manual* is important because Coleridge's decision here to approach the problems of Christian society through the qualities of the Bible transforms traditionally "literary" questions—the nature of the text and its interpretations, the relationship between author and text—into primary means of approaching the ultimate problems of mediating between finite and infinite, individual and society, past and present. As a consequence, it becomes increasingly possible for Coleridge to view his own poetic experience, however negative, not as a sign of his isolation and failure but as a measure of the intimacy and intensity of his participation in the problems shaping life in his times.

At one point in *The Statesman's Manual*, Coleridge remarks that "The misery of the present age is that it recognizes no medium between the literal and metaphorical." That is to say, it recognizes no clearly defined medium between the belief that things are literally themselves, admitting of no translation and thus requiring no interpretation, and the belief that nothing exists except by virtue of its being translated into something else—hence, everything is interpretation. If, as the former proposition implies, the world is absolutely resistant to generalization, then our desire to know and to understand and the reason and imagination of which we are so proud are necessarily irrelevant in the order of things. The world, a complacent multitude of self-contained and self-defining unities, answers (or, rather, fails to answer) every question we put to it with a massive indifference. On the other hand, if things are infinitely generalizable, then all identity is lost, and the sense of distinct reference that gives form and focus to our questionings dissolves into a Protean and undifferentiated chaos, an idiot witness answering every question in the affirmative. Unless metaphor (or, let us say, the figurative) lurks somewhere as an attribute of the external world, then there can be no meaning. Unless there is a literality somewhere in the heart of the seemingly infinite play of figures and the interpretations they imply, there can be no truth—no preference for one meaning over another.

It was, according to Coleridge, because the skeptical eighteenth century lacked a solution to this problem (or, rather, forgot that a solution existed in the right understanding of the Bible) that men gave themselves over to an unprincipled expediency, grounded in despair and resulting in the alternative waves of revolt and repression threatening to wreck society.

Coleridge believes that man's confusion about his place in the order of things is the result of his position as both subject and object of his own consciousness. Coleridge gains his own most immediate experience of the problem through his difficulty, reflected in the poetry, in accepting the consequences of the distinction between the author writing and the work written or, to put it another way, between the unarticulated conviction of selfhood and the often anomalous manifestations which are its only literality. In the act of writing, the poet possesses his creation, and it cannot bear witness against him. Possessing it in the anticipation, he relinquishes it in the achievement. Confronting his own completed poetry, the poet faces something which is at once his own creation and something shockingly alien to him. The poem is no longer malleable and responsive to the flow of his thoughts and feelings. He has moved on and left the poem behind, an object

92    to testify that he has not always been as he now sees himself, asserting its authority to define him to the world more clearly, more concisely, than he can define himself. So the author writes on in order to avoid being "represented" by what he has written and in order to reaffirm the priority, the privilege, of the writer over writing itself.

But Coleridge had to face the problem of what happens when a poet virtually stops writing poetry. For such a poet to try to continue in the same relationship to what he has written (a self-enhancing, possessive relationship) is to risk becoming a living parody of his own creations (the Coleridge of the popular imagination) or, even worse, an embarrassment to his own poetic greatness (like the Wordsworth of the later years). Coleridge's own crisis of poetic identity moves him to question whether the author is really "authorized" by the comprehensiveness and continuity of his creativity, as God is God by virtue of the perpetual act of creation that is one with the continual affirmation of identity, the infinite "I AM." He concludes that it is folly to place the full weight of aspiration, if not for divinity, then for greatness; if not for greatness, then for legitimacy; on the individual self—so fragile a vehicle even for the normal business of living. Besides, such a view ignores the fact that the enterprise of writing goes on even when there are no great writers to "authorize" it. Nor will the argument suffice that writing is sustained in the absence of immediate greatness by a traditional canon, for, as Coleridge suggests, the tradition—our Judaeo-Christian tradition—is already begun before the first author writes; it begins with the Bible—a text, constitutive of all possible acts of authorship because its source is not an author but pure authority. Thus, the tradition begins not with an author but with a text to be interpreted, and every subsequent text expresses its own understanding, its own interpretation, of its origin—of the authorship immanent within it. But all these texts (and all conceivable texts) remain well within the boundaries of the enterprise initiated by the Bible because each must establish its authority with reference to something else; only in the Bible are authorship and authority one and the same. In this context, authorship is less an attribute of individual personalities, less the origin of texts which serve in turn as pretexts for interpretation, than it is the mode of interpretation privileged in a tradition originating with and informed by the Bible.

Coleridge begins *The Statesman's Manual* by arguing: (1) that the Bible is unique in the "fact of its immediate derivation from God"; and (2) "that the interment of such a treasure in a dead language must needs be contrary to the intentions of the Gracious Donor" (*SM*, 7). The first point immediately establishes the source of the Bible's authority, and the ultimate literality to which everything in it refers, in its unique identity as the Word of God. At the same time, however, the second point argues the translatability of that uniqueness. Thus, the Bible itself provides the instance of the interpenetration of the literal and metaphorical to which Coleridge's definition of the symbol (also a part of *The Statesman's Manual*) refers.

According to Coleridge, the symbolic experience of the world originates in God's earliest, miraculous revelations of himself:

> In the infancy of the world, signs and wonders were necessary to break down that superstition, idolatrous in itself and the source of all other idolatry, which tempts the natural man to seek the true cause and origin of public calamities in outward persons, circumstances and incidents: in agents therefore but surges of the same tide, passive conductors of the one invisible influence, under which the total host of billows, in the whole line of successive impulse, swell and roll shoreward; there finally, each in its turn, to strike, roar and be dissipated. (*SM*, 9)

To the complacent literal-mindedness of natural man, content to create hierarchies of cause and effect without ever contemplating the preconditions making such a relationship possible, God answers with a counterliterality, undeniable yet contradictory. Miracles and wonders represent the entry into our awareness of an inward aspect of the world's existence, of an immanence or in-being. Coleridge goes on to say that "with each miracle worked there was a truth revealed which thenceforward was to act as its substitute"

94 (*SM*, 9). In other words, the literal miracle becomes a sign or a figure for the truth of which it makes men aware: that there is a presence, one of whose attributes is a literality capable of participating in but not limited by the literality of the sensible world. Thus, through the infinite translatability of the Bible, both in language and in time, this anomalous revelation, intimating an inwardness immanent in the literal, is simultaneously that which originally sets in motion, continues to set in motion, and serves as the ideal goal of the continuous process of translation—of the displacement in the direction of the more meaningful and the more true—of which the play of figuration and the ongoing task of interpretation are equally a part.

Once this awareness is introduced into man's experience of the world (which is the same as saying, once man becomes aware of his own inwardness), it becomes pervasive and

> gives birth to a system of symbols, harmonious in themselves, and consubstantial with the truths, of which they are the *conductors*. These are the Wheels which Ezekiel beheld, when the hand of the Lord was upon him, and he saw visions of God as he sate among the captives by the river of Chebar. "Whithersoever the Spirit was to go, the wheels went, and thither was their spirit to go: for the spirit of the living creature was in the wheels also."
>
> (*SM*, 29)

Ezekiel's vision of the unity of temporal history with the movement of God's spirit in the world is at the center of Coleridge's conception of the ongoing immanence of the Bible in the culture whose origin it marks. He elaborates:

> The truths and the symbols that represent them move in conjunction and form the living chariot that bears up (for *us*) the throne of the Divine Humanity. Hence, by a derivative, indeed, but not divided, influence, and though in a secondary yet in more than a metaphorical sense, the Sacred Book is worthily entitled *the* WORD OF GOD.

Hence too its contents present to us the stream of time continuous as Life and a symbol of Eternity, inasmuch as the Past and Future are virtually contained in the Present. According therefore to our relative position on its banks the Sacred History becomes prophetic, the Sacred Prophecies historical, while the power and the substance of both inhere in its Laws, its Promises, and its Comminations. In the Scriptures therefore both Facts and Persons must of necessity have a twofold significance, a past and a future, a temporary and a perpetual, a particular and a universal application. They must be at once Portraits and Ideals.

(*SM*, 29–30)

The truths of the Bible are thus not abstractions from history but continue to dwell within it. Therefore, whatever can be comprehended as historical is simultaneously appropriated to biblical history and to these truths—they are infinitely generalizable. In this light, postbiblical history must be seen not as a movement away from origins, in which the play of figure on figure, interpretation on interpretation, places us at an ever-increasing distance from any literality that might guarantee the value of such enterprises; rather, it is seen as our collective effort, generation by generation, to expand ourselves to fill the creation marked out for us by the Bible. That this space is so vast that all our history and all our works have not been sufficient to occupy it or even to intimate its limits is comprehended here in the distinction between the WORD OF GOD and the Sacred Book: "by a derivative, indeed, but not divided, influence, and though in a secondary yet in more than a metaphorical sense, the Sacred Book is worthily entitled *the* WORD OF GOD." Here then is the ultimate referend of the problematical relationship of author and text—a problematic capable, in Coleridge's view, of generating a culture and of swallowing it whole.

For all these reasons, Coleridge claims:

The Bible alone contains a Science of *Realities*: and therefore each of its elements is at the same time a living GERM, in which the Present involves the Future, and in the Finite the Infinite exists potentially. The hidden mystery in every, the minutest form of existence, which contemplated under the relations of time presents itself to the understanding retrospectively, as an infinite ascent of Causes, and prospectively as an interminable progression of Effects—that which contemplated in space is beheld intuitively as a law of action and re-action, continuous and extending beyond all bound—this same mystery freed from the phenomena of Time and Space, and seen in the depth of *real* Being, reveals itself to the pure reason as the actual immanence of ALL in EACH. (*SM*, 49–50)

It is the Bible that comprehends within itself and makes possible what mere science mistakenly considers fundamental modes of apprehension (this then is at the heart of the "Method" essays). More immediately, Coleridge's view of the Bible and his corollary view of history make it possible to see that the incomplete and unsatisfactory nature of all figurative acts does not find its cause in the defective creative will of the author; rather, it refers to the very heart of figuration—our continuous enterprise to extend ourselves, to match ourselves to the fullness of being intimated in the Bible.

For all of this, the rhetoric of *The Statesman's Manual*, often strained and obscure even by Coleridgean standards, remains somewhat at odds with the meaning he is trying to convey. Moving back and forth from the language of theology to that of philosophical idealism, he strains to write about what is immanent in writing itself, occasionally reaching for a rhetorical peak at odds with what is most essential in his meaning: that the Bible and its truths are the continuing substance of our lives and not a detachable essence. What finally anchors his enthusiasm is the substance of the Bible as a book:

If it be the word of Divine Wisdom, we might anticipate that it would in all things be distinguished from other books, as the Supreme Reason, whose knowledge is creative, and antecedent to things known, is distinguished from the understanding or creaturely mind of the indi-

vidual, the acts of which are posterior to the things, it
records and arranges. (*SM*, 18–19)

We might anticipate that it would be distinguished from all other books, and it is; yet it is still a book—a text that can be shared and taught, and thus used to reconstitute the unity of principle which provides the basis for harmonious social existence. Coleridge's sense of the intellectual and spiritual fragmentation at the root of social conflict is reflected in his discussion of the new reading public (*SM*, 36–39). This public, sharing little or nothing in terms of educational background, lacking that "sound book learnedness into which our old public schools continued to initiate their pupils" (*SM*, 39), has not only corrupted itself with the cheap thrills provided by novels but is also seen to be easy prey for every ideamonger to come along. In Coleridge's view, the intellectual rootlessness of these readers makes them the natural allies (or dupes) of a paradoxically complacent eighteenth-century skepticism; and their confidence in their own uneducated taste is catered to by those unscrupulous individuals trying to evade the effective censure of educated men and women. In part, *The Statesman's Manual* is a call for those who share a common, traditional intellectual background to recognize their own potential importance and responsibility to arrest the steady diffusion of intellectual authority, which is simultaneously destroying the commonwealth and the commonwealth of letters.

The text with which Coleridge's man of "clerkly acquirements" (*SM*, 36) is expected to arrest this process of diffusion is, of course, the Bible. The social reasons for this choice are obvious: by showing that virtually every lesson taught by the myriad political writers and historians of the time is already contained in the Bible, Coleridge hopes to reunite the fragmented social, intellectual, and moral aspects of life with reference to a single overarching authority. Properly understood, the Bible could provide a central, generative authority by which the true nature of contemporary ideas, events, and opinions might be known. Of course, such a scheme would require interpreters, who would make it their business to accommodate present events to the terms provided by the Bible. Ideally,

98 the boundaries of interpretive freedom would be guaranteed by the interpreters' common intellectual and educational backgrounds. A social order guaranteed by the textual order of the Bible constitutes the program of *The Statesman's Manual*. The central difficulty of such a program is to provide terms for the understanding of the Bible which make clear the ways in which its authority extends beyond the bounds of religion, as it is normally understood.

To this end, Coleridge pits the Bible (as an instrument of historical self-understanding) against the dominant, utilitarian mode of historical analysis. The supreme reason, he argues, immanent in the Bible, is constitutive of all experience—it makes experience, rather than a chaos of sensations, possible. Understanding, on the other hand, is a response to, and thus is limited by, the immediacy of experience. For this reason, understanding can never stand in a truly explanatory relationship to the phenomena of which it is a part, and experience can never be a sufficient ground of truth. Its dependence on the understanding constitutes the basic weakness of that mode of historical analysis finding the ultimate causes of actions and events in individual motives, the most fundamental of which is expediency (Coleridge has in mind Hume's *History of England*). As Coleridge points out, man makes the motive, not the motive the man, and what is a motive to one is no motive to all to another (*SM*, 21). So the problem of what makes motive—a discernible relationship between what is thought or known and action —possible remains. The immediate harmony of knowledge and action is the distinguishing attribute of the Bible—the text in which comprehension compels active belief.

Even if we can occasionally explain discrete events in terms of such motives of expediency, Coleridge argues, this does not explain how in a "well-governed society the contradictory interests of tens of millions of such individuals may neutralize each other and be reconciled in the unity of the national interest" (*SM*, 21). What binds expedient creatures together into a society is the immanence of principle and the ideas that are its vehicles:

> How else can we explain the fact so honorable to Great Britain that the poorest amongst us will contend with as much enthusiasm as the richest for the rights of property?

These rights are the spheres and necessary conditions of free agency. But free agency contains the idea of freewill; and in this he intuitively knows the sublimity, and the infinite hopes, fears, and capabilities of his own nature.

(*SM*, 18)

As we have seen, not only does the Bible contain all possible principles underlying all possible motives to all possible actions; it also creates the very possibility of a phenomenal world informed by principle or idea when it interrupts the complacent literality of natural being. Since the primary act of faith in reason, the constitutive faculty, contains "the possibility of every position to which there is any correspondence in reality" (*SM*, 18), since this primary act of faith is enunciated in the word God, and since Scripture is the vehicle of this supreme reason in the world, it is to Scripture that we must look for the ultimate causes of the society and history that it makes possible.

Clearly, one of the implications of this view is that the Bible constitutes the possibility of all future texts and all possible readings of those texts because it is only through the Bible that the intention to write, to produce a text, means for us what it does, indeed, means anything at all.[1] Like the historical event, a poem, for example, can be seen as the result of an intention. But the intention to write a poem and thus to be a poet is hardly self-explanatory. Such an activity must exist as a possibility before anyone can intend to do it, and here lies the inadequacy of the traditional model of literary authority based on a canon of the "greats." All those works have authors and hence human intention—a motive— behind them, which, however thoroughly articulated, is not sufficient either to explain or to justify them. Ultimately, in such a model, the authority guaranteeing the enterprise, justifying the introduction of still another book or poem into a world already

---

[1] In other words, it functions as a transcendental signified, implying all possible manifestations of its signifier, text. In the case of the Bible, origin and reflection are one and the same, and it is the biblical model of the text which paradoxically defines origin as an originary act of reflection or revision. Fichte's thetic judgment, as interpreted by Paul Ricoeur, argues much the same thing for the *Cogito Sum* (*Freud and Philosophy: An Essay on Interpretation*, trans. Denis Savage [New Haven: Yale University Press, 1970], p. 43).

crowded with them, must be the superiority of the author, created and maintained in conflict with other authors. What results is a kind of family history—a genealogy of the gods—full of incests, fratricides, patricides, etc., but not a society of letters or a literary history with a discernible relationship to or role in the larger society and its history.

We can now begin to see how the analysis of the Bible in *The Statesman's Manual* promotes the understanding of history and, implicitly, of the history of the text, as the fundamental mode of our historical existence, and moves Coleridge, in *Biographia* and later works yet to be discussed, toward the reconstitution of his own authorship in order to promote a more genuinely fraternal society of letters and a more genuinely historical literary history.

# 5

## *BIOGRAPHIA LITERARIA* AND
## "TO WILLIAM WORDSWORTH":

### Poetry and the Priority of
### Interpretation

The intimate relationship between *The Statesman's Manual*'s concern with miraculous revelation and the biblical text and the eccentric form of *Biographia Literaria* is succinctly expressed (in quite a different context) by Herbert Schneidau in his discussion of the Old Testament miracles:

> Yahweh is not incarnated in the appearances, nor do they function as symbolic keys to him: they are neither continuous with him in any sense, nor analogous to his essence. The 'cosmic continuum' is deliberately broken, the forms are arbitrary signals, and the arbitrariness is the point.[1]

Without much effort, these observations about miraculous revelation can be translated into a series of questions particularly appropriate to *Biographia*. In what sense is the man present/absent in what the author writes, even if he is writing about himself? To what degree is the arbitrariness of any textual order its point? Are we to conclude that meaning becomes possible only at that point where apparent form, apparent order, dissolves into an awareness of the arbitrary? Certainly few books can seem more arbitrary than

[1] Herbert N. Schneidau, *Sacred Discontent: The Bible and Western Tradition* (Baton Rouge: Louisiana State University Press, 1976), p. 141.

102 *Biographia*; and we must recognize that it is the arbitrariness with which a staggering diversity of materials present themselves as equally representative of Samuel Taylor Coleridge that poses the book's challenge to Coleridge and, through him, to his readers.

As *Biographia* progresses, any attempt to sustain an autobiographical, self-allegorizing narrative becomes increasingly peripheral to a diversity of philosophical, historical, and literary discussions. In so far as the book may be considered a reply to Wordsworth's "Growth of a Poet's Mind," it implies that the diversity of that mind is too great to be contained within any one form of discourse. This difference further suggests that Coleridge is not so much interested in validating one identity over another as in reconciling the conviction of identity with the diversity of competing, sometimes contradictory, voices in which it finds expression. Coleridge's refusal to adopt a single voice raises the question of whether there is any necessary correspondence between the relations among mental contents and among the discourses in which they find expression. Consciousness, seeking its own literality in discourse, is brought to face the fact that if it is not to remain a kind of pure contingency, it must address itself to its own inability to make one voice, one Word, suffice when many are available. Thus, Coleridge identifies as prior to the Wordsworthian problem of poetic vocation the problem of the vocation of consciousness itself.

Both Wordsworth and Coleridge have a great deal at stake in their literary autobiographies because, for both men, identity is closely tied to vocation—knowledge of that activity peculiarly appropriate to the individual. Wordsworth's sense of vocation issues in a poetic voice that subsumes all others. The multiplicity of voices heard in *Biographia* suggests that identity emerges not out of a Wordsworthian resolution into a single voice but out of the mutual interrogation and revision of many voices. For Coleridge, the personal voice—the voice associated with the events and experiences of an individual life—is not necessarily privileged over the less personal voices that the self assumes. In *Biographia*, the boundary between the distinct individual and the philosophical, historical, and religious materials of culture is much more problematical —even more problematical than his relationship with nature or with his own past.

At the very end of *The Prelude*, Wordsworth achieves the prophetic conviction of his vocation and, at the same time, finds the voice proper to that conviction. Coleridge's definitions of imagination and fancy, the culmination of Volume I, offer no such revelatory, self-confirming convergence of concerns with prophecy, identity, voice, and vocation. The consecration of the moment as revelation, so familiar in Wordsworth, is almost completely lacking. The burden of the revelation as personal event is borne by the letter from a friend, while the definitions stand apart, speaking *propria impersona*. Nevertheless, their appearance in *Biographia Literaria* argues that the definitions *are* personal statements. The Coleridgean emphasis falls not on the subsumptive power of poetic discourse, nor even on the subsumptive power of a more impersonal philosophical discourse, but on the emergence of a voice that appears to speak directly out of its subject matter—a voice immanent in self *and* in culture.

Given the way in which the letter from a friend transforms *Biographia* XIII into a sort of anticulmination, displacing Volume I's philosophical concerns into the realms of literature, religion, and biography, it should come as no surprise that Volume II's extended discussion of Wordsworth reaches a premature (because it comes a chapter before Coleridge's summary of Wordsworth's characteristic defects and beauties) culmination in what appears to be a digression—a chapter innocuously titled "Remarks on the Present Mode of Conducting Critical Journals":

> I know of no claim that the mere opinion of any individual can have to weigh down the opinion of the author himself; against the probability of whose parental partiality we ought to set that of his having thought longer and more deeply on this subject. But I should call that investigation fair and philosophical in which the critic announces and endeavours to establish the principles he holds for the foundation of poetry in general, with the specification of these in their application to the different classes of poetry. Having thus prepared his canons of criticism for praise and condemnation, he would proceed to particularize the most striking passages to which he deemed them applicable, faithfully noticing and as faithfully distinguish-

ing what is characteristic from what is accidental, or a mere flagging of the wing. Then if his premises be rational, and his conclusions justly applied, the reader, and possibly the poet himself, may adopt his judgement in the light of judgement and in the independence of free agency. If he has erred, he presents his errors in a definite place and tangible form, and holds the torch and guides the way to their detection. (*BL*, II, 85)

Of course Coleridge has been defining his canons of criticism since the beginning of the book (perhaps most prominently in chapters I and XIV), and, thus, this statement establishes his right to make the judgments contained in the chapter to follow. But Coleridge goes farther, raising explicitly the question of who has authority over a work already written—a question present at every stage of his discussion of Wordsworth, the implicit burden of which is that the greatest poet of the day cannot accurately describe the nature of his own poetry. It is in this context that Coleridge grants the poet's authority in matters of opinion, which he carefully distinguishes from judgment, effectively circumscribing that authority within the realm of "mere" opinion. The still more subtle argument implicit in that first sentence consists in the assumption that the poet's engagement, perhaps even responsibility, does not end with the writing of the poem. He is involved with his readers because, in the wake of poetic creation, he becomes a reader himself, his new distance from what he has written suggested by the fact that he has an opinion about it, rather than simply possessing it as his own. The ambiguity of the poet's relationship with what he has written suggests an equally ambiguous relationship with his own talent. This talent he wishes to regard as an attribute of his person; yet his difficulty in holding on to what he has written —the instability of the relationship between creator and created— challenges the security of his talent and the reality of his poetic election.[2] The problem is much exacerbated by the absence of the

[2] Michel Foucault discusses the author as the victim of his own writing in "What Is an Author?" in *Language, Counter-Memory, Practice: Selected Essays and Interviews by Michel Foucault*, ed. Donald F. Bouchard (Ithaca: Cornell University Press, 1977).

authority of a defined canon and of the stability of an audience perceived to be much like himself. In the world of the reviews and of the new reading public, the poet's security in the identity of poet, as well as his reputation, is more and more dependent on his role as a reader of his own poetry.

The poet's reading of his own work does indeed reflect a parental partiality and falls within the realm of mere opinion because it is more a stance than an interpretation. It is by means of this stance that individual poems are "revised" and absorbed into a more general abstraction, "my poetry," which merges into the poet's perception of himself, giving it weight and substance in his own mind and in the minds of others. The poet might represent his poetry to himself and to his public as a revolutionary gesture, as a hedge against the decline of values, or as an expression of a heroic, if tortured, individualism. As the poet becomes less and less confident that he knows to whom he is writing, as the traditional means by which writers educate their readers and predispose them in their favor apply to a smaller and smaller part of the reading public, the poet's means of influencing his public become more and more obtrusive, and he grows less and less willing to allow the poem to mediate, unaided by a carefully calculated poetic persona, between the author and reader.

The Romantics were the first great poseur poets of the modern age, and a public equally unsure about the men who wrote for it clutched eagerly at the clues provided by poetic personae. In his concern over the reviews and over the rise of the reading public, Coleridge expresses his fear that the figure of the poet, the idea of poetry, might become more compelling than poetry itself.

When Coleridge grants that the poet's opinion is the best possible, context transforms the concession into a warning against taking the poet at his word. The poet's opinion is an extension of his personality, but, for Coleridge, the meaning of literature resides not in its relation to personality (that is, as expression) but in its relation to value. The critical method described by Coleridge is a stance, defining the nature of literature as clearly as the poet's persona seeks to define the nature of his poetry. Through the figure of the interpreter, Coleridge argues that the meaning of poetry as an activity is that all experience, as well as all knowledge, is intimately concerned with value. Coleridge's concern with judgment refers less to judgment about the quality of the poem that is the end of the process than to the intermediate judgments distinguishing the characteristic from the accidental, choosing appropriate examples, and formulating and applying principles. These mediate judgments define the possibility of value judgment. The real importance of the critic resides in his concern with constituting the possibility of value through the implicit interpretation of sufficiency involved in every critique.

The notion that interpretation is mediate in nature is not likely to startle anyone, even if we extend it to claim that interpretation defines the nature of mediation itself. However, to argue that interpretation at once defines the mediate and, in its form, constitutes the true nature of poetry is an entirely different proposition, for it is to suggest that poetry is no less mediate than interpretation. It suggests that although poetry may be the pretext for interpretation, it is not its origin, which is to say that although poetry may be prior to interpretation, it is not the authority for interpreting. We may conclude from this that the supposed priority of poetry is itself an interpretation, suggesting that interpretation chooses poetry to be prior and cannot accurately be regarded as an extension of poetry, which we can take or leave alone as we choose.

Poetry too is mediation, and as we saw in our discussion of *The Statesman's Manual*, Coleridge regards poetry and interpretation as having a common source in the need to define the terms upon which mediation is possible at all. In fact, in Coleridge's view, interpretation is if anything prior, choosing poetry to define the terms of its priority. The point behind Coleridge's reading of the Bible is that no priority is adequate to establish authority, and thus he seeks to detach the notion of priority from the assumption of privilege. In the Coleridgean reading, human priorities are in themselves ultimately irrelevant with regard to the question of authority since the absolute nature of God's authority precluded all other conceptions of authority until he created the possibility of mediation in the Bible—the text without pretext. In this act of divine fiat, God offers interpretation as the form of mediation and thus "authorizes" mediate definitions of authority, not as substitutes for his own but as mediate interpretations of it. Thus, for Coleridge, both poetry and interpretation have their origin in God's originating unnatural act.

The new journals, like the new reading public, represent to Coleridge a fundamental and sweeping change in the conditions under which works are written and read. As we remember it, Wordsworth's "Preface" to *Lyrical Ballads* paints a picture of the true poet circumscribed by ill-conceived rules of poetic composition and surrounded by hacks cranking out verse in accordance with an arbitrary poetic diction. Agreeing with Wordsworth about the depressed state of poetry, Coleridge adds to the Wordsworthian scenario the increasing power and influence of journals which have not yet risen above the expression of opinion, often motivated by personal or party interest. Furthermore, the growth of a reading public with nothing in common but a desire to read meant the decline of the ideal of the more or less homogeneous literary commonwealth, which had made such a thing as poetic diction effectively possible.

It was neither desirable nor possible to keep people from reading, but how could so large and diverse a group be absorbed into literary culture without becoming its tyrant? Recognizing that literature and literary knowledge could not continue on the same terms (for one thing, because the majority of the readers were socially and intellectually unprepared to accept its authority), Coleridge also saw that Wordsworth's contempt for the notion of a special body of poetic knowledge would leave literature at the mercy of the mass reading public by depriving literary men of their primary means of educating readers to their own taste.

Before the rise of this new reading public, it was possible for writers to pretend to write to each other. And in an educational system where every man was a poet (or poetaster in classical verse anyway), it was possible to pretend that to define the poet was also to define the reader of poetry. But in a reading public where few read in order to write themselves, the problem of defining the reader, or at least of erecting some kind of mediating structure between the author and the public, was pressing indeed. Merely to redefine the poet as his own most important reader, perhaps his only important reader, was a solution threatening to deprive poetry of its social function and to isolate "serious" literature from normal social activity.

For Coleridge, the critical journals, for all their faults, indicated the direction that literary culture would have to take.

108     Their very existence reflected the public's desire for literary guidance, though not necessarily for the literary education which is the only ground of taste. But in dealing largely with interested opinion, these journals showed little interest in elevating the public; rather, they descended to its level in order to enlist its numbers in support of their own influence. Presenting themselves in the guise of literary authority, their excesses and the manifest arbitrariness of their views must eventually discredit literary authority in the eyes of a public whose credulity would reach its inevitable limit. But the journals, their practice modified by a rational, responsible criticism, also suggested a way in which the unruly public might be tamed and the world of the arts brought back to some semblance of order.

What stands between Wordsworth and an accurate description of his own poetry, between opinion and judgment, between the practice of the journals and true criticism, is a paucity of concepts particularly appropriate to the reading (as opposed to the writing) of literature, or, to put it differently, a deficient sense of literature as an independent force, an ontological or historical category in its own right. One of the things with which Coleridge struggles in *Biographia*, one of the things at stake in his wrestlings with Wordsworth, is something less accurately described as a new idea of literature than as the new idea of Literature itself—the ultimate consequence of the intensifying literary self-reflectiveness of the eighteenth century, described by Bate in *The Burden of the Past and the English Poet*.[3]

Literature emerges from *Biographia* as more than the sum of its parts, more than great authors and great works. Instead, literature is seen as a vast and constitutive activity/environment, working out its own progress in history through the simultaneous efforts of authors, critics, journalists, thinkers, publishers, patrons, readers, etc. The insistence with which the Coleridge of *Biographia* maintains the conviction of identity, even as he pursues it through its many discursive forms, is the analogue of his conviction that the idea of literature exists as the sustaining bond between a staggering diversity of ideas and concerns. Once the notion is accepted that the critical journals represent as properly literary a phenome-

---

[3] Walter Jackson Bate, *The Burden of the Past and the English Poet* (Cambridge: Harvard University Press, 1970).

non as the poetry of Wordsworth—so obviously in the Great Tradition—it is no longer possible for a poet or poem to represent the
literature of the age.

Coleridge sees quite clearly that individual works and their
authors are no longer defining literature; rather, literature as an
idea is influencing, perhaps even determining, practice as never
before. The age is not dominated by a poet who, in effect, writes
in his poetry the next chapter of the tradition but by the idea and
awareness of literature. Such considerations call into question certain basic assumptions about the Romantic period. For instance,
they suggest that poetry is not the key to the age, only its greatest
achievement. Part of the self-validation achieved by Coleridge in
*Biographia* resides in his ability to sustain this apparent contradiction in his treatment of Wordsworth (that is, Wordsworth is the
greatest poet of the age, but the key to the age is in the interpretation, not the poetry). This powerful distinction between literary
history or awareness and poets or poems is manifested in the book's
very first chapter when Coleridge substitutes, for the purposes of
his own literary history, William Lisle Bowles for Milton as the
most significant source for the understanding of his (Coleridge's)
poem "Religious Musings."

In *Biographia* I, the chapter most concerned with the
origins of Coleridge's career, he presents himself as *choosing* to
attribute poetry priority. He distinguishes himself from Wordsworth
in Volume II by questioning the idea that poetry is somehow privileged with regard to nature. In Coleridge's view, Wordsworth's relationship with nature can in no way account for the poetry, much
less authorize it. Indeed, one of the chief differences between the
Wordsworth of *The Prelude* and the Coleridge of *Biographia* is
that Coleridge's account finds its causes within the realm of
poetry and philosophy, not in terms of a unique relationship with
nature. For Coleridge, poetry too is unnatural. This creates some
special problems for the reader of *Biographia* because Coleridge is
simultaneously justifying his *choice* of poetry to be prior, often
using language distinctly reminiscent of Wordsworth's "Preface,"
and refuting Wordsworth's conclusion that poetry *is* prior. We are
in perpetual danger of failing to realize what Coleridge is about
when he is engaged in dissociating Wordsworth's arguments from
his conclusions. In Volume II, Coleridge makes use of many

110    Wordsworthian ideas about the value of poetry and praises Wordsworth's poetry itself as a means both of justifying and of defining
the ethical choice, the fundamental judgment of value, implicit in
his choice of poetry as the pretext for interpretation.

Speaking of "Religious Musings" in *Biographia* I, Coleridge questions whether the thoughts of the poem do not require a
degree of attention unsuitable to poetry and complains of his own
misguided attempts to give poetic coloring to "abstract and metaphysical truths" (*BL*, I, 2–3). The suggestion is clear that, in this
poem at least, there is a fundamental incompatibility between poetry
as an expression that calls attention to itself as poetry (that is, as a
kind of language associated with the intention to write and to be
understood in a certain way) and poetry as a vehicle for ideas or as
an instrument of knowledge. The great fault of "Religious Musings"
*as a poem* is, according to Coleridge, the subordination of the
former function to the latter. Coleridge faults himself for having
misunderstood the nature of poetry, but the conclusion to be drawn
from his critique is that poetry is inadequate to comprehend within the limits of its formal intentionality the "abstract and metaphysical truths" associated with knowledge.

Coleridge uses "Religious Musings" to illustrate what he
regards as the great flaw in his early thinking—his tendency to
exercise the understanding without awakening the heart—and
credits William Lisle Bowles, of all people, with saving him from
aimless metaphysical speculation, ungrounded in the "truths of the
heart" (*BL*, I, 7–10).

Taken *in toto*, this account has a number of interesting
implications. For one thing, Bowles, even in Coleridge's own time,
must have been a pretty slender reed upon which to lean a whole
career. The idiosyncratic nature of the claim, its apparent arbitrariness, emphasizes the impression that he *chose* Bowles, and through
him poetry, to be his pretext. It is certainly hard to believe that
Coleridge was seized by the greatness of Bowles, as we might imagine someone seized by the greatness of Milton or Shakespeare.
Bowles's poetry was important because it helped him to define
what was missing in his intellectual life, and Bowles is chosen
here to represent that absence.

We have already heard Coleridge's opinion that "abstract
and metaphysical" truth is somehow inimical to the nature of

poetry. The truth which Coleridge regards as appropriate to poetry is the "truth of the heart," which Coleridge came to see was the necessary basis for productive speculation about abstract and metaphysical truth. It is important to recognize that poetry is both valued and confined in this notion of the truths of the heart, and it remains to be seen whether it has gained more than it has lost in the arrangement. We should also note that it would not be at all correct to conclude from this account that poetry is prior to knowledge as it is usually defined (or, rather, as it is characterized as "abstract and metaphysical truth"), for Coleridge fixes on Bowles because his speculations have prepared him to do so and because their future success demands it. True, the truths of the heart are seen as prior to the truths of the intellect, but this is not the same as arguing that poetry is prior to interpretation. Coleridge is saying only that poetry bears a special relationship to the truths of the heart—a conclusion reached through a prior act of interpretation. In fact, it is the nonpoetic logic of Coleridge's intellectual development that chooses poetry as its own necessary pretext.

But what is a truth of the heart anyway? Clearly, it is more experiential, more intuitive than other truths, and the phrase "truths of the heart" suggests that it is largely, though not exclusively, a form of self-knowledge. These truths of the heart would seem to bear a special relation to experience, but Coleridge's account of how he chose Bowles as a necessary part of his intellectual development suggests that the truths of the heart bear a special relation to the self's experience of itself and not, for example, to nature. Coleridge's argument tends toward the conclusions that poetry is not privileged with regard to nature or experience and that poetry does have some special relationship with the self's experience of itself. The implication is that poetry refers to and finds its authorization in the needs of the self and not in nature, and therefore is no less unnatural than interpretation.

Coleridge's truths of the heart are retrospectively established as prior in response to the intellect's recognition of an absence. In some ways, this appears to be a psychological revision of his philosophical distinction between reason and understanding in *The Statesman's Manual*. There reason is seen as that faculty (also an act of faith in itself, indistinguishable from being) which constitutes the possibility of experience whereas understanding is seen as the faculty operating after the fact of experience to order and comprehend. The similarities with Coleridge's account of his early development are substantial since, for Coleridge, the truths of the heart appear to constitute the possibility of the truths of the intellect. Perhaps it would be more accurate to say that the truths of the heart represent a knowledge, perhaps more intuitive than other knowledge, of the internal constitution which defines the possibilities and limitations of experience and intellect alike. But whether we are speaking of reason or of the truths of the heart, it will not do to forget that our knowledge of these sources of experience and intellect is the result of "normal" interpretation's discovery of an absence at its center and of its choice of a pretext to fill that void.

The nature of *Biographia* as a literary and intellectual project casts some additional light on this problem since the message of the book is, in part, that Coleridge's early experience and the poetry he wrote then are important because of what examining them can help us to know. In fact, we would not be exaggerating Coleridge's implicit position here by saying that all previous experience and all previous statement, poetic or otherwise, are valuable only insofar as they lend themselves to interpretation and yield knowledge, and that the only statement which is regarded as an expression of truth is the present one (or, rather, the present statement subsumes the truth of all previous statements into itself). For Coleridge, this view has the great virtue of making sense of his own career, emphasizing its division into two parts: a poetic career in which his achievement had faltered and been surpassed by Wordsworth, and a newer philosophical-critical career into which his own and Wordsworth's earlier work were being subsumed. Ultimately, Coleridge's present statement, *Biographia Literaria*, *grants* poetry priority for its own nonpoetic reasons, also managing to suggest that because it is poetry (that is, because of the role it has been assigned), it cannot serve as a sufficient instrument of knowledge without compromising its own value as poetry.

*Biographia* I culminates in Coleridge's statement of two fundamental poetic aphorisms: first, that genuine poetry is not so much that which we read with pleasure as that to which we return; and second, that "whatever lines can be translated into other words of the same language without diminution of their significance, either in sense of association or in any worthy feeling, are so far vicious in their diction" (*BL*, I, 14).

The first of these aphorisms seeks to establish a qualitative difference between reading and rereading, the experience and the return. There are two choices involved here: the choice to read and the choice to return. In a sense, the initial choice is always blind—an act of faith conditionally attaching value to the act itself in the absence of any knowledge of its outcome (that is, in the absence of any knowledge of the real nature of the choice). The initial choice is a willed discontinuity from "normal" activity, and the return folds this discontinuity back on itself, comprehending it and reestablishing continuity on new, revised terms. A continuity cannot, by definition, comprehend its own end and, therefore, for all intents and purposes, it has no meaning. However, an act sufficient to arouse the conviction of discontinuity bears a special relationship to the continuity. It is quite possible to comprehend the extent of a discontinuity, for it need only be long enough to establish the fact of its discontinuity. In the return, it is possible to comprehend the discontinuity as a distinct phenomenon, in all its discontinuousness, the object, of course, being to determine the nature of the continuity through an understanding of what is sufficiently discontinuous.

But what is the "continuity" about which we are growing increasingly abstract? In one sense, it is the continuous process of intellectual development recounted in *Biographia*. The discontinuity in terms of which that process may be comprehended is Coleridge's decision not just to write poetry but to be a poet. In a more general sense, the continuity is the continuous act of interpretation which supports consciousness and constitutes the possibility of experience whereas the discontinuity is poetry itself. Thus, the return is the a posteriori act of interpretation which reconstructs the continuity out of the terms of the poem's discontinuity.

The implications of such a model are considerable. For one thing, it argues against the notion that interpretation is a break in the continuity of poetic discourse. It may be argued that there is a continuous tradition of poetic discourse, composed of poets and poems speaking to and about each other, but it cannot fairly be concluded from this that interpretation may be *sufficiently* regarded

*114* as a willful (perhaps even perverse) interference in this continuity.[4] For from what may well be an even more fundamental point of view, the "continuity" of the poetic tradition is a series of discontinuities, springing from and answering to the continuous development of interpretation ("interpretation" here being defined as that instrument which constitutes the possibility and limits of knowledge at any given time).

That interpretation should appear to the poet as a perverse interference (and that critics who regard themselves as poets *manqués* should apologize for perversely interfering) is entirely natural, for the poet, insofar as he is a poet (and the critic insofar as he is a poet), exists within that bounded continuity sufficient to define discontinuity. In order to clarify this somewhat, let us return to the specific case of *Biographia Literaria*. One of the curious things about that book, as a literary biography, is how very little it has to say about Coleridge's poetry or about his career as a poet "from within," as it were. If we apply the implications of Coleridge's *Biographia* account to *Biographia* itself we can retrace Coleridge's own revision of his career. In the beginning, that is, in the real beginning, we have a young Coleridge who both writes poetry and speculates in abstract and metaphysical truths, partly out of natural inclination and partly because, after all, that is what he was taught to do in school. Writing "now," sometime between 1815 and 1817, he claims to "remember" that he chose poetry for intellectual reasons (that is, the necessity of pursuing the truths of the heart). But we should stop and ask ourselves if we really believe this, not as the prelude to proving or disproving it but because the question is necessary and expected of us. We are also aware that for some time early in his career Coleridge wrote poetry, very good poetry, and regarded himself primarily as a poet. When Coleridge remembers how, in effect, he came by process of interpretation to regard poetry as prior to interpretation in relation to truth, this invites us to recognize, in the absence of any "inside" account of his poetry and career, that when Coleridge chose to consider himself a poet, he blinded himself to the pretext for that choice and literalized the conviction of poetry's priority in the fiction "I have always been a poet." Surely this is one reason for Wordsworth's prominence in Volume II, for

[4] See Harold Bloom, *The Anxiety of Influence* (Oxford: Oxford University Press, 1973).

behind the Wordsworth of the "Preface" stands the Wordsworth of
The *Prelude*, making exactly that claim and representing, in part,
the Coleridge who is being revised in *Biographia*. In this relationship between Coleridge's original choice to become a poet and his
consequent forgetting of the origin of that choice, and his "remembering" of that choice and consequent forgetting that he ever forgot it, we have an excellent example of the "folding-over" that we
have been discussing. But the folding-over and return to the larger
interpretive continuity carry with them a trace of what they undo:
the return represents, even as it undoes, the discontinuity which
determines its form. Thus, in a remarkably clear case of folding-
over, Coleridge substitutes in his anecdote about his old teacher,
James Bowyer, "I was always possessed of the convictions I now
hold about the nature of poetry" for "I was always a poet." In
the conspicuousness of its absence, Coleridge's poetry (in the few
pages in which he does speak of it, Coleridge treats his poetry as
if it was strictly a juvenile phenomenon) is very much like Holmes's
"dog who did not bark in the night"—an absence pointing to a
presence.

      Coleridge's Second Aphorism—"whatever lines can be
translated into other words of the same language without diminution of their significance, either in sense of association or in any
worthy feeling, are so far vicious in their diction"—raises a question
which has lurked in the background of our discussion for some
time now—that of repression. According to this aphorism, good
poetry establishes a unique relationship between poetic diction
(what is actually written) and intention (what is meant). In poetry,
we are told, the experience of one word should not be translatable
into the experience of another, even if the two words are theoretically synonymous. This may or may not be true, but the fundamental issue with which the aphorism is concerned is not so much
whether an analogy can be drawn between poetry and experience
as with the true nature of their identity, if any. (Interestingly,
Coleridge leaves moot the all-important question: is the poem,
insofar as it is regarded as an experience like other experiences,
not a poem at all, but merely another experience?)

      The implications of the aphorisms differ substantially, de-
pending on whether or not we regard experience as prior to understanding. But Coleridge made it clear in *The Statesman's Manual*

that reason constitutes the possibility of experience (although Coleridge concedes that experience necessarily *appears* to constitute the possibility of understanding). So, even as he draws his implicit analogy between poetry and experience, Coleridge deconstructs it, revealing that the one is like the other, not in the justice of its claim to priority but in its blindness to its own essentially a posteriori nature. In our daily lives we tend to behave as if the experience of the other was constitutive of all else—a fact of which Coleridge complains bitterly. This forgetting is necessary if we are to maintain our faith in our own reality; for with that perversity which in itself almost defines the human, how can we be comfortable in a world the possibility of which we ourselves constitute? The problem arises when, in order to act intelligently, it becomes necessary not to experience but to understand the nature of experience—that is, to remember. Coleridge's aphorism places poetry within this general context by pointing out the specific act of forgetting involved in writing a poem: forgetting that the poem was not always as it is now, in its finished form.

"Kubla Khan," along with its famous preface, is perhaps the most complete and complex documentation in the Coleridge canon of his concern with the necessity of not remembering if the poet is to function as poet. The relationship between poem and preface that suggests not only that the poem is incomplete but that the poem is not a poem (that is, the product of conscious artifice) is itself an expression of the powerful repression of the poet's awareness of the actual history of his poem and of the consequent displacement of that awareness onto sometimes highly rationalized fictions of poetry and composition. Paradoxically, the insistence that the poem "is and has always been" is closely related to the conviction of its incompleteness. In composition and revision, the poet seeks to involve his language as fully as possible in his intention, and if his intention guides his choice of language, it is equally the case that, through this process of selection and substitution, the language serves to define the intention. Thus, in a sense, the poet writes in order to discover what he means. Yet it is also the case that in coming to know what he means, the poet also comes to know that he does not mean what he has said. For the poet too, at least phenomenologically speaking, understanding always *succeeds* writing, and thus the poem is outdated by its own meaning.

The claim that the poem has always been as it is expresses this sense of incompleteness because it serves to disentangle the poet's understanding of his intention from what he has actually written, both as the necessary prelude to writing again and as the basis for a revised notion of his identity as poet. But this fiction also serves to repress the poet's knowledge of his failure to fill the mental space implied by the poem as it was being written. The fiction argues the sufficiency of the poem *as poem*; that is, it argues that the poem *invokes* the intention of the author without sufficiently defining it. What we have then, from the point of view of the poet, is an instance of the self's failure to apprehend its own nature satisfactorily through its own creation. Self-understanding is, in a very important sense, seen as incidental to the writing of poems, for no "argument from design," based on the completed poem, is possible.

The implication of all this, and certainly one of the implications of the preface-poem relationship in "Kubla Khan," is that being a poet (that is, the conviction of one's identity as a poet) and writing a poem are not necessarily compatible. The poet's generalized sense of himself as a poet makes it possible for him to write poems that are recognizably his, but it also threatens to turn his poems into self-parodies. His individual poems are theoretically the basis of his identity, but each one resists the generalization necessary to integrate it into his poetic identity. With each descent into language, the poet risks everything, for he is all too aware that his own words can contradict and betray him. He must insist that his poem is sufficient for everyone else (as Coleridge does for "Kubla Khan"), but his survival as a poet depends upon his own conviction that it is insufficient for himself.

No poet possesses a sense of his identity as poet except by virtue of his willingness to renounce the sufficiency of his individual creations and generalize them into what amounts to an interpretation. This interpretation does not supply a reading of his poems in a critical sense so much as it uses the materials provided by the poems to develop a personal rationale that is also a myth of the poet and his powers. No poet can write except by virtue of repressing his knowledge that he is a poet only because of his skill as an interpreter. The poet exists as poet by means of an almost continual repression: repressing the knowledge that he invented himself as a poet, repressing the full awareness of how his poems were written,

118 and even by repressing his knowledge of the poems themselves. Consequently, he faces an almost constant threat of the return of the repressed. He fears this return—it is the source of much of his anxiety about himself and his poetry—but he also welcomes it, for, in a way, the point of it all, the thing that makes it worthwhile, is the return.

It was not lost on Coleridge that, in poetry, we never seem to learn anything that we do not already know (at least insofar as poetry addresses sensation)—that we do not discover new things so much as remember things that we have forgotten or recognize them in a new guise. This is the special nature of poetic knowledge: knowledge repressed in order that it may be rediscovered, perhaps even renewed, in the experiencing rather than in the knowing. There is great risk in such repression, for what we know can return in strange and unexpected forms, tempting us to deny what we know and thus to deny ourselves (or the world around us). Poetry is the *diaspora* of knowledge for, just as knowledge-interpretation gathers the disparate into the center, poetry disperses the center out to the periphery; and at no time is it entirely certain whether this dispersal is an exile or a conquest.

As we have seen, the more closely we interrogate Chapter I, the more elusive its substance, both as a beginning to this book and as an account of the origins of Coleridge's career. What is clear is that the chapter's greatest obfuscation—the insistence that Bowles, not Milton, has the most to teach us about "Religious Musings"— has a programmatic significance: it would seem to argue that the shift from poetic values, the family romance of the Great Tradition, to the interpretive values associated with the idea of literature (which become explicit in Chapter XXI) is already underway as Coleridge is about to begin his period of greatest poetic productivity. Thus, his poetic development and his growth away from poetry become one and the same—not the stopping of one career and the beginning of another but the working out of a single continuous concern for literature. The importance of this substitution for our modern understanding of Coleridge (and for Coleridge's understanding of his own career) is indicated in these remarks from Geoffrey Hartman's "Reflections on the Evening Star: Akenside to Coleridge," which presents a brilliantly compressed articulation of the problematic presently governing Coleridge studies:

A belated poet rejoices in the symbols and accoutrements *119* of his tradition. They fill his verses with a presence rarely as frigid as Akenside's. But Coleridge is representative of a sadder ending. He is afflicted by secondariness as by a curse: his relationship to writing of all kinds is more embarrassed than that of Keats and more devious than that of Akenside. His imagination sees itself as inherently "secondary"—not only because it follows great precursors in poetry and philosophy (though that is a factor) but chiefly because of the one precursor, the "primary Imagination . . . living power and prime agent of all human perception . . . repetition in the finite mind of the eternal act of creation in the infinite I Am." His religious sensibility, conspiring with a burdened personal situation, makes him feel at a hopeless remove from originality.

That Coleridge was deeply disturbed by the priority of others—and of the Other—is hardly in question. Too much in his life and writings reflects it. It can be argued that he was, in his way, as "counterfeit" a poet as MacPherson or Chatterton. He had done better perhaps to invent new origins, as they did, than to be echo and imitate imitations in a perverse sacrifice to divine primacy. His poetry shows to what extent he *shrinks* into creation, like Blake's Urizen.[5]

Although it could hardly be better observed in its particulars, Hartman's argument is distorted throughout by an implicit judgment against Coleridge—a condescension in the names of Milton, Blake, and Wordsworth that infects his study of poetic belatedness with Hartman's own critical nostalgia for the Great Tradition. Despite his disclaimer, the negativity of Hartman's view of the secondariness implicit in the primary imagination is based on an analogy with the quite different *poetic* secondariness of Coleridge's relation to Milton and Wordsworth. In the light of their poetic ambitions, a Blake, a Milton, or a Wordsworth might be "embarrassed" by the primacy of divine creativity, but not, I think, a Coleridge.

[5] See *New Perspectives on Coleridge and Wordsworth: Selected Essays from the English Institute*, ed. Geoffrey H. Hartman (New York: Columbia University Press, 1972), pp. 111–12.

120     The "originality" of Milton or Wordsworth is, by definition, exceptional, and a concept of literary value based exclusively on analogies with such achievements is as profoundly inhumane as an ideal placing no value on any creativity that is less than infinite. Coleridge also sees quite shrewdly that to give such weight to achievements that transcend the human norm is to make those achievements meaningless or, like comparisons with God, simply irrelevant. Of course, Hartman is quite right when he says that much of what Coleridge wrote betrays a sense of the burden of secondariness. It is also true, however, that Coleridge never stopped trying to define the terms upon which the literary value he sensed in his own work could be defined, even if he was not a Wordsworth, a Milton, or a Kant. This need to define the value of all that writing and all that thinking that is not of transcendent value, and to identify the perspective from which it can be related to the works of the Great Tradition, determines the importance of the analogy of divine creativity which replaces the analogy of poetic greatness in the later work.

Milton, Blake, and Wordsworth are poets whose sense of prophetic (as opposed to historical) identity is based on a firm conviction of the immanence of vocation in personality. The achievement of a sense of vocation may be seen as a depersonalization or depsychologization of biography. If, as Hartman says, the minor poet makes of poetry the sublimation of loss (a nostalgia for the tradition from which he is a permanent exile), then the great poet feigns the sublimation of personality into history, making of poetry a depersonalization seeking to establish (perhaps even feign) the immanence of a self-confirming authorial identity in the "history" that he writes. This is finally to impose an "immanent," authorial self on literary history, sublimating other aspects of personality and history at once into an immanent, authorial identity that places the highest value on the redemptive powers of the creative will.

Milton's simultaneous sublimation of biography and pastoral in "Lycidas," Blake's similar treatment of Genesis in *The Book of Urizen*, and Wordsworth's treatment of epic in *The Prelude* are examples that suggest themselves. Of Coleridge's poems, perhaps "Religious Musings," significantly enough, offers the clearest contrast. Its subtitle, "A Desultory Poem, Written on Christmas Eve of 1794," seems in its hint of self-deprecation to deny, even as it solicits, comparison with Milton's "On the Morning of Christ's Nativity." In that poem, Milton locates himself in the closest possible anticipation of the incarnation of Christ—the last prophet. He succeeds in maintaining a properly religious humility even as he is sublimating the incarnation into his own poetic enunciation. First and foremost, Milton's concern is with his own prophetic voice as he seeks to locate himself just this side of the border separating poetic from divine prophecy. The vast distance that the radical Puritan Milton posits between himself and God works finally to make of the penultimacy of Milton's prophecy an irrelevancy.

As Richard Haven has noted,[6] Coleridge makes of his poem an attempt to rationalize the sublime and to historicize the prophetic. Emphasizing in his notes the basis of the poetic vision in contemporary history and philosophy, Coleridge concerns himself with the historical identity of prophecy rather than with the prophetic identity of history. As a result, we get not the voice freed to speak prophetically in a prophetic moment but a voice burdened and confused by the antimyth of history. Attempting to establish in the here and now the perpetual historical identity of Christ and of biblical revelation, Coleridge finds himself without the voice necessary to animate the vision. Rehistoricizing Christ humanizes him:

> . . . Thou Man of Woes!
> Despised Galilean! For the Great
> Invisible (by symbols only seen)
> With a peculiar and surpassing light
> Shines forth the image of the oppressed good man.
>
> ("Religious Musings," lines 8–12)

Humanizing and historicizing the myth undercuts Coleridge's poetic just as intensifying the myth enhanced Milton's. To put it another way, in a poetic context, to humanize is to reduce. The career that Coleridge chronicles in *Biographia* does indeed begin from "Religious Musings," with Coleridge's discovery of the

---

[6] Richard Haven, *Patterns of Consciousness: An Essay on Coleridge* (Amherst: University of Massachusetts Press, 1969), pp. 100–01.

*122* essential inhumanity of poetic greatness and his awareness of the
need for a broader concept of literary value, based not on the questions Who said it? Is it good or bad? but on the as yet implicit
question What does it mean?

Coleridge's apparent reluctance to accept poetic incarnation, his desire to remain firmly rooted in history, suggests in its
contrast with Milton that an awareness of literature as such is not
perpetuated by great poets (indeed, it may represent a way of thinking about literature that is foreign to them) but by those who, in
their difficulty or inability to block the intrusion of the frail personality, of a history-burdened self, make of themselves the chief
interpreters of poetic greatness. To a degree even more radical than
Hartman suggests, Coleridge's writings can be seen as a striving
after the negative apotheosis of poetic greatness. The conclusion
that we are invited to draw from such a conception of Coleridge's
work is that poetry culminates not in great poets but in tradition
itself—that literature is the last and greatest of poets.

The substitution of Bowles for Milton in *Biographia* I also
serves to represent or interpret the much more important substitution of *Biographia* itself for the pivotal 1807 poem "To William
Wordsworth, Composed on the Night After His Recitation of the
Poem on the Growth of an Individual Mind." If "On the Morning
of Christ's Nativity" serves as Milton's enunciation, then "To William Wordsworth," with its Lycidean references, serves as a Coleridgean enunciation of a quite different kind. Ostensibly a hymn
of praise, the poem intensifies appreciation until it emerges as a
creative force in its own right, and Coleridge becomes the priest
overseeing, perhaps making possible, Wordsworth's assumption of
poetic greatness.

"Into my heart," Coleridge begins, "I have received that
Lay / More than historic, that prophetic Lay "(lines 2–3). Not
just a history of his own development, Wordsworth's poem becomes
through his investigation of "the foundation and the building up /
Of a Human Spirit" (lines 5–6) prophetically true for all men. This
process of self-realization tends toward "what within the mind /
By vital breathings secret as the soul / Of vernal growth, oft quick-
ens in the heart / Thoughts all too deep for Words!" (lines 8–11).
Surely it is a curious thing to say of a poem—that it speaks of things

too deep for *words*. The statement serves to point up the necessary incompleteness of the genuinely prophetic poem, redefining the prophecy and its fulfillment away from Wordsworth's previous life and the achieved poetic vocation of *Prelude* XIV, toward a fulfillment outside the poem in the self-recognition occurring in the heart of the reader.

The degree to which the ultimate possession of the poem is shifting from poet to reader is apparent when Coleridge goes on to suggest that there is a limit to Wordsworth's understanding of his own poem, marked by a tendency to mistake "The light reflected as a light bestowed" (line 19). Indeed, the line seems to hint at some connection between Wordsworth's poetic greatness and the limited nature of his self-knowledge.

In the first fifty lines or so, Coleridge offers a descriptive summary of Wordsworth's poem, which develops into an extraordinary piece of verse criticism, culminating not in Wordsworth's poetic enunciation but in a dense vision of vision contemplating itself in the form of hope:

> For thou wert there [in France], thine own brows garlanded
> Amid a mighty nation jubilant,
> When from the general heart of human kind
> Hope sprang forth like a full born Deity!
> —Of that dear Hope afflicted and struck down,
> So summoned homeward, thenceforth calm and sure
> From the dread watchtower of man's absolute self,
> With light unwaning on her eyes, to look
> Far on—herself a glory to behold,
> The Angel of the Vision!

> (lines 33–43)

We recognize in this account Wordsworth's disillusionment when the liberty of the early revolution gave way to persecution and violence; and we are reminded of his return to England, convinced that no historical, external change could sustain or realize a vision-

124 ary hope. And, to anticipate, we recall how Wordsworth succeeds in *Prelude* XIII (in 1805) in reuniting a visionary hope, sustained by imagination, with this world.

However, these lines are not about Wordsworth but about hope, who shifts our attention to herself initially through an arresting ambiguity: it is not precisely clear whether the "dread watchtower of man's absolute self" is a France in which a potentially apocalyptic human desire has not only freed itself from artificial restraints but has abandoned natural limitation as well, or whether it is the defense to which a disillusioned Wordsworth withdrew. Both views have their application, and, taken together, they make of the line's ambiguity a suggestion of Wordsworth's own ambivalence, perhaps confusion, concerning the possible contradictions between his aims and prophetic stance.

In *The Prelude*, Wordsworth retrospectively understands the failure of the French Revolution as the result of a separation of human desire from the nature in which it finds its proper limitation and definition. This separation results in a negative, if limited (that is, "merely" historical), apocalypse. In this sense, the poet of nature works to hold back the apocalypse toward which imaginative desire naturally tends. But Wordsworth's withdrawal from the political/historical is also a withdrawal into the self. This withdrawal is not absolute, vitiated as it is by the presence of Dorothy and of Coleridge, but Wordsworth ends his poem in a position unmistakably above and apart from, rather than among, his fellow men—almost as if he does not know how to get down from Mount Snowdon. Despite his desire to speak prophetically to his fellows, the absolute nature of his prophetic stance, tied to his determination to avoid being involved once again in the tides and turmoils of history, prevents Wordsworth from coming down from the mountain and returning, transformed, to social life. Instead of becoming a redeeming message, the prophecy remains an ark for two. Coleridge's ambiguity thus emerges as a suggestion that there is a defensiveness in the prophetic stance that prevents the prophecy, if not from being heard, from being read aright if accepted on its own terms.

In this way, focus is shifted to the incompleteness imposed on Wordsworth's prophecy by his stance. The shift away from the terms of Wordsworth's self-understanding is reinforced and given additional definition by echoes from Milton's "Lycidas," which serve to elicit from Wordsworth's poem Coleridge's own revision of its prophetic significance. "Look / Far on," "Summoned home-ward," and "The Angel of the Vision" echo Milton's famous lines: "Where the great vision of the guarded mount / Looks toward Namancos and Bayonna's hold; / Look homeward Angel, melt with ruth" (lines 161–63).[7] Michael, or the faith militant, gazing out on the Catholic strongholds of England's enemies, is asked to relax his stern vigilance long enough to feel pity for Lycidas. Michael's is the prophetic stance, dating from the Old Testament, of God's people embattled in a temporal struggle which can lead them to mistake a kingdom in this world for the prophesied king-dom of God. Milton calls Michael's attention to the New Dispen-sation (the primary paradigm for the prophetic revision of proph-ecy), in which a personal salvation born of love subsumes into itself a national salvation born of law. To shift terms around a bit, Milton asks Michael to come down from his mount (or watch-tower) in order to recognize a more intimate, human prophecy.

Milton avoids the divisive militancy of Michael's prophetic stance by his elaborate guise of pastoralism, in which subsumption of the prophetic into the self-deprecating he follows the example of his savior. Wordsworth, Coleridge seems to say, cannot relax the tension necessary to sustain his own prophetic stance. The nature with which Wordsworth has invested so much of his own imagina-tion is no longer sufficiently independent to counter the isolating movement of prophecy.

"Lycidas" makes of this strategy a defense of poetry—an answer to the implicit question "What good is it?"—by tying its resolution to the admission that poetry is but a "dally[ing] with false surmise" (line 153). The evidence of faith is beyond sensa-tion and, therefore, if representable at all, becomes available only through the mediation of that which is known to be unreal, with-out valid natural analogy. Pastoral serves Milton's prophetic pur-pose because it is frankly artificial and because it presents little resistance to prophetic allegorization while allowing Milton to avoid the defensiveness of an overtly prophetic stance. Thus, the

[7] John Milton, *Complete Poems and Major Prose*, ed. Merritt Y. Hughes (New York: Odyssey Press, 1957).

same strategy that allows Milton to avoid confining his prophecy within the limits of natural analogy allows him to bring Lycidas, his prophetic identity established, back to this world to be the genius of the shore.

Coleridge's point is not Wordsworth's inadequacy as a poet—after all he is engaged in raising him to the pantheon of the Great Tradition as Milton's complement, the extender of what Milton saw as the intimate prophecy of the New Dispensation into the New Dispensation of the epic of self. No, Coleridge's point is that in the process of completing his great task, Wordsworth necessarily forgets (and entices us into forgetting) how much of Milton he is leaving out. The restoration of this knowledge to the reader, and to the literary awareness of the time, requires a stance quite different from that of the Great Poet. A prophetic stance necessarily ignores whatever resists assimilation, and just as Wordsworth must "leave out" much of Milton, it was necessary for Milton to ignore the truths given voice in his classical sources.

For Coleridge, the failure of Wordsworth's hopes to find their fulfillment at the end of *The Prelude* is inherent in the relationship between his defensive propheticism and what it reveals of his continued insistence, however disguised, on the absolute nature of the self. (It is not out of place here to observe that in his own attempts to discuss poetry, Wordsworth was always forced back on the character of the poet, in sharp contrast to Coleridge's attempt to separate principle from personality.) Out of this combination of reference and suggestion comes Coleridge's own version of the restoration of hope. Looking "Far on," she becomes herself a vision to behold, the "Angel of the Vision," sustaining the rebirth of hope. The vision that hope strains to see is, it would appear, a vision of herself. Thus, it is the turning of vision on vision, of prophecy on prophecy, that converts it from a self-referential act into something to be perceived by others, a text, and thus active among men in this world. Hope's peculiar stance, both alienated and involved, is echoed in Coleridge's own visionary contemplation of a prophetic voice from which he is at great pains to distinguish himself. Coleridge counters the prophetic exclusivity of Milton and Wordsworth alike through his own visionary apprehension of the simultaneity of the poetic tradition.

"O great Bard!" creates the author out of Wordsworth the

man or, more accurately, out of the poem. And Coleridge proceeds
to install Wordsworth in his own vision of literature as something
distinct from and larger than individual poets and their works:

> I viewed thee in the choir
> Of ever enduring men. The truly great
> Have all one age, and from one visible space
> Shed influence! They, both in power and act,
> Are permanent, and time is not with them,
> Save as it worketh for them, they in it.
>
> (lines 48–54)

This is not a great poet's notion of his own position. Wordsworth
wishes to subsume and supersede Milton, not to coexist with him
in the single time and place created by Coleridge's intense appreciation and awareness of the simultaneity of literature. Not only that,
but "ere yet the last strain dying awed the air" Coleridge saw the
"great Bard." In effect, he beats Wordsworth to the conclusion of
his own poem and now proceeds to go beyond Wordsworth's conception of the fulfillment of his poetic vision.

As Coleridge contemplates the timeless simultaneity of
the Great Tradition, he feels hope (presumably the corollary of the
"joy" that was so injured in "Dejection") rekindle:

> The pulses of my being beat anew:
> And even as Life returns upon the drowned,
> Life's joy rekindling caused a throng of pains—
> Keen pangs of Love, awakening as a Babe
> Turbulent, with an outcry in the heart;
> And fears self-willed, that shunned the eye of Hope;
> And Hope that scarce would know itself from Fear;
> Sense of past Youth, and Manhood come in vain;
> And all which I had culled in wood-walks wild,
> And all which patient toil had reared, and all,
> Commune with thee had opened out—but flowers

Strewed on my corse, and borne upon my bier
In the same coffin, for the self-same grave!
That way no more! . . .

(lines 62–76)

The very return of hope brings with it a throng of self-reproaches about his waste of his own talents. These self-reproaches are imaginatively transformed, along with all which "Commune with thee had opened out," into flowers strewn on the coffin of the Coleridge who was. In this way, the poem turns back once again to "Lycidas," and Coleridge becomes both Lycidas and the author of his own visionary elegy. With "That way no more!", an obvious echo of Milton's triumphant "Weep no more!" (line 164), Coleridge follows Milton in transforming the retrospection of elegy into prophecy, announcing the death of the old Coleridge, burdened by a sense of alienation from his own identity as a "great" (that is, Wordsworthian) poet and the birth of the Coleridge of "To William Wordsworth." This new stance or identity is above all interpretive, stressing the humane value of *not* being a great poet in its emphasis on the values of the "listening heart."

As if to stress the peculiar powers of this position, Coleridge goes on in the final twenty-one lines to do precisely what Wordsworth's stance prevents him from achieving: Coleridge's prophetic moment culminates not in the confirmed superiority or enforced isolation of the prophetic speaker, but in a "happy vision of beloved faces" (line 107). As Wordsworth stops speaking, the intensity of Coleridge's listening perpetuates the effect of Wordsworth's voice beyond its actual limit, revealing that the origin of this special moment is in Coleridge's capacity to respond at least as much as in Wordsworth's poetic power. When a balance is struck between speaking and listening, when hearing becomes as important as speaking (perhaps more important than speaking), then speech is transformed into prayer. For Coleridge, prayer, rather than the more militant, self-enhancing stance of Wordsworth, becomes the paradigm for a new propheticism.

With "thy deep voice had ceased—yet thou thyself / Wert still before my eyes," Coleridge reminds Wordsworth that the prophecy must inevitably end and the voice reassume its identity as a man. On this human ground, it is the Coleridge who speaks *to* men, not the Wordsworth who speaks above them without really believing in them, who is truly prophetic. In order to enunciate this "new" stance, Coleridge reaches back before the period of his most intense personal and compositional involvement with Words-worth toward a more original, more distinctively Coleridgean stance: a prophetic intensity of appreciation, born of an awareness of standing aside from the Great Tradition in order to appreciate it as such and of an accepting awareness that he is finally reluctant to pay the price of being taken up into that tradition. Perhaps the best example of such an early poem is "Lines: On an Autumnal Evening," begun in 1792, which begins with Coleridge checking the flight of fancy into visionary anticipation:

> O thou wild Fancy, check thy wing! No more
> Those thin white flakes, those purple clouds explore!
> Nor there with happy spirits speed thy flight
> Bath'd in rich amber-glowing floods of light;
> Nor in yon gleam, where slow descends the day,
> With western peasants hail the morning ray!
>
> (lines 1–6)

This wariness, lest fancy carry one too far, too fast is also a prominent theme in "Monody on the Death of Chatterton," where Coleridge is primarily concerned with the self-destructiveness of allowing fancy to turn back upon itself, enhancing the poetic identity even as it renders it fatally vulnerable. In "Lines: On an Autumnal Evening," Coleridge combines this notion of the destructiveness of poetic self-enhancement with the larger themes which Hartman has treated so well in his essays, "Reflections on the Evening Star: Akenside to Coleridge" and "Blake and the Progress of Poesy."[8]

8 See *New Perspectives on Coleridge and Wordsworth*, pp. 85–131; and Geoffrey H. Hartman, *Beyond Formalism: Literary Essays 1958–1970* (New Haven: Yale University Press, 1970), pp. 193–205.

Fancy unrestrained would carry Coleridge from his present position, bidding the sun farewell, to the western peasants, with whom he would be in a position to greet the sun. Coleridge's reluctance to exchange belatedness, nostalgia, for anticipation—surely a more prophetic, more poetically charged position—can, in the terms that Hartman has provided, be seen as a reluctance to be taken up into the perpetual westering of the sun or noontide of the poetic spirit. Choosing to remain behind, Coleridge distinguishes himself from the self-perpetuating and self-involved movement of poetic greatness, insists on remaining a man tied to time and place rather than a spirit and, as the next lines suggest, opts for retrospection over anticipation:

> Ah! rather bid the perish'd pleasures move,
> A shadowy train, across the soul of Love!
> O'er Disappointment's wintry desert fling
> Each flower that wreath'd the dewy locks of Spring,
> When blushing, like a bride, from Hope's trim bower
> She leapt, awaken'd by the pattering shower.

> (lines 7–12)

Gazing on the sunset in a spirit of retrospection rather than anticipation, Coleridge is burdened by an intense sense of loss, which is both an expression of personal regret and a recognition of the natures of pastness (an awareness of things gone) and of presentness (an awareness of impending loss, of an experience receding even in the experiencing—like the sunset). All this raises the obvious question: if past and present are so burdened, why is Coleridge so reluctant to abandon them? The answer seems to lie in the possibility of sharing the past and even the present—a possibility abridged if not lost in the difficulties of sharing a state of visionary anticipation. Remaining embodied, clinging to a human if burdened situation, it is at least possible to come together for the funeral.

Strewing Miltonic flowers on the grave of his hopes, Coleridge succeeds in suggesting that his renunciation makes possible an intimate meeting and greeting that would be drowned out by a more powerful, more strident poetic voice. This muted reference to "Lycidas" is particularly appropriate because the "false surmise" offered in that floral offering refers most immediately to the absence of a body to serve as the focus for a common sense of loss.

It is important that we recognize the significance of Coleridge's use of his "burdened" situation at such an early age—a theme we are used to encountering in the later poetry, when his situation truly was burdened. The absurdity of a boy of twenty talking about the end of his hopes is manifest, and it seems likely that here at least Coleridge is experimenting with a stance, perhaps even a poetic program. All this should call into question the ease with which we are accustomed to assume that when these themes appear in the later poems their significance is literal and biographical. It seems equally reasonable to argue that when he is truly burdened, when he is truly in need of resources, he reaches back to a poetry in which the burden is a stance, a metaphor, as a way of countering its literality and subduing it to an artistic and intellectual order. If much of Coleridge's life seems to literalize those early metaphors, it makes a certain sense to reach back in order to transform the literal once again into metaphor. "Lines: On an Autumnal Evening" is itself suspended between the polar identities of its own central image. If the sunset is just a sunset, then literality becomes a terrible trap. If the sunset is "really" a metaphor, then the poet is disenfranchised, having lost not only the world's but his own literality.

At this point, Coleridge turns to a retrospective vision of his own spring, of his emergence and half-confirmation by the seasonal spirit of his own youthful potential. Pursuing this "Dear Deceit," he follows the ideal of himself, tracing her footsteps "on the accustom'd lawn," and marking "her glancing mid the gleam of dawn." The personified maid, spring, who first arises amid the gleam of the sinking sun and then becomes associated with the dawn, is, in this doubleness, Hesperidean. The evening star thus marks the dawn of a new day, the origin of which is in the belatedness of the sunset—Hartman's *abendland* over which the half-light of the moon presides:

132

> When the bent flower beneath the night-dew weeps
> And on the lake the silver lustre sleeps,
> Amid the paly radiance soft and sad,
> She meets my lonely path in moon-beams clad.
> With her along the streamlet's brink I rove;
> With her I list the warblings of the grove;
> And seems in each low wind her voice to float
> Lone-whispering Pity in each soothing note.

> (lines 29–35)

Coleridge goes on to embower the newly discovered identity of his female entity, pity, envisioning himself almost as her
Pygmalion:

> She speaks! and hark that passion-warbled song—
> Still, Fancy! still that voice, those notes prolong.
> As sweet as when that voice with rapturous falls
> Shall wake the soften'd echoes of Heaven's Halls!

> (lines 52–55)

Pity calls the poet away from his own visionary/fanciful speech,
enjoining him as Milton enjoins Michael, to turn to a softened
vision of his prophetic role. This turning away from the full light
of poetic/prophetic ambition is emphasized in Coleridge's conception of his own embowering role: "A flower-entangled arbour I
would seem / To shield my Love from Noontide's sultry beam"
(lines 59–60). Pity must be shielded from the noontide of poetic
ambition and prophetic militancy because she is the child of a softened, listening poetic stance. Indeed, to return to Coleridge's "Still,
Fancy!", it becomes clear that the poem turns on the difficulty of
speaking and listening at the same time and defines itself as a
seeking after an alternative poetic stance, characterized by the
oxymoron, listening speech. This movement of the poem culmi-

nates in a role reversal in which Coleridge himself is "taken up"
into the heavens, not in self-enhancement but as an extension or
sublimation of his devotion to his antiprophetic or listening muse.

From this point, Coleridge turns again toward recollection and regret. But in light of his vision, his dismay at returning
to the "real" world gives way to a memory that feeds joy, not regret.
Thus, memory becomes a positive presence and no longer a re-
minder of absence:

> Dear native brook! like Peace, so placidly
> Smoothing through fertile fields thy current meek!
> Dear native brook! where first young Poesy
> Stared wildly-eager in her noontide dream!
> Where blameless pleasures dimple Quiet's cheek,
> As water-lilies ripple thy slow-stream!
> Dear native haunts! where virtue still is gay,
> Where friendship's fixed star sheds a mellow'd ray,
> Where Love a crown of thornless Roses wears,
> Where soften'd Sorrow smiles within her tears;
> And Memory, with a Vestal's chaste employ,
> Unceasing feeds the lambent flame of joy.
>
> (lines 81–92)

But, Coleridge admits at line 92, this union of "native brook" and
poetic noon is "No more," and the poem reemerges into the physical
twilight, confessing its disenfranchisement, both from its own past
and from the perpetual futurity of the westering spirit:

> Scenes of my Hope! the aching eye ye leave
> Like your bright hues that paint the clouds of eve!
> Tearful and saddening with the sadden'd blaze
> Mine eye the gleam pursues with wistful gaze:
> Sees shades on shades with deeper tint impend,
> Till chill and damp the moonless night descend.
>
> (lines 101–06)

134   Coleridge has finally emerged into the pure present of his poem, in which the sunset is both an image of his own life, accumulating tint on tint in its westering toward death, and a promise. For night, however chill and damp, is not death. Presentness is a point from which past and future are envisioned as complementary absences—the point of possibility the cost of which is an intense awareness of absence and for which, in this poem, there is as yet no proper rhetoric.

This sense of presentness as an absence or betweenness, in which one falls silent, is reinforced in the passage's echo of the conclusion to *Paradise Lost*, in which Coleridge and the "eve" which defines his condition become indeed the new Adam and Eve: "So spake our Mother Eve, and Adam heard / Well pleas'd, but answer'd not. . . . Some natural tears they dropp'd, but wip'd them soon" (lines 624–25, 645). It is the simultaneity of the present, the presence of "tint on tint," and the absence of a stance or language to express that presence, toward which Coleridge points.

The line of development binding together "Lines: On an Autumnal Evening," "To William Wordsworth," and *Biographia* defines as a problem of stance or voice what was more destructively seen in the Mystery Poems as an irresolvable psychic division within Coleridge the man. There is no question that such divisions existed, but this redefinition of the main line of his development allowed him to feel that his art was not a vehicle of this division, that it was once again possible to distinguish art and man. This view implies that his involvement with Wordsworth was, in some sense, an excursus or digression, necessitating the assimilation of this powerful presence to the new definition—a task accomplished beginning with *Biographia* XIV, the first chapter in Volume II.

# 6

## IMAGINATION AS TEXT:

### Poem and Object in *Biographia* XIV

Coleridge commences Volume II, and his extended discussion of Wordsworth, with a new, revised beginning. This is
particularly appropriate because his association with Wordsworth
was indeed a new start. But by this time in his career, as I suggested
in the last chapter, Coleridge is coming to see the new start as a
mistaken path. Coleridge's critique of Wordsworth is also a critique
of his own self-misunderstanding and an attempt to win back from
Wordsworth (and from the Coleridge of that period) a renewed
understanding of his proper vocation. To a substantial degree, this
redefinition has already been achieved in Volume I, but Wordsworth remains the formidable test (text?) of Coleridge's recovered
powers.

Chapter XIV, at first glance confusing in the variety of
its subject matter, recapitulates the progress of Volume I, trans-
lating its concerns into terms more directly applicable to Coleridge's
relationship with Wordsworth. Instead of Bowyer, Bowles, and
"Religious Musings," the new point of origin is the planning of
*Lyrical Ballads*. The "fundamental aphorisms" of Chapter I are replaced by the "cardinal points," through which Volume I's philosophical concerns with subject-object relations are translated into
a concern with the identity of the poem as utterance and as object.
And like Volume I, Chapter XIV culminates in a famous definition
of imagination.

*136*    Chapter XIV divides itself into two main parts: an account of the genesis of *Lyrical Ballads* and an attempt at "philosophical" definitions of a poem and of poetry. In the first part, Coleridge begins by recalling the two cardinal points of poetry which were the substance of his literary discussions with Wordsworth: (1) the power of exciting sympathy by adherence to the truth of nature and (2) the power of giving the interest of novelty by virtue of the modifying colors of imagination (*BL*, II, 5).

Coleridge's cardinal points are strongly reminiscent of the classic double-bind of mimetic theorists: how is it that a poem is both recognizably like and recognizably unlike its object? [1] Whatever else may be indicated by the difficulties of those seeking a sufficient definition of poetry in the concept of *imitatio*, they certainly suggest that the possibility of poetry is determined by the possibility of likeness without identity (here I mean by "identity" merely to name the quality of being identical). Coleridge translates this possibility, as he so often does, into the language of response, with the identity of the poem and its object corresponding to sympathy—an assent which is both a recognition and an engagement—and with their difference corresponding to novelty. The nature of the relationship between difference and identity is clarified by the relationship between novelty and sympathy, for novelty is a response which necessarily comprehends a knowledge of the norm, of the already-recognized, which is the basis of sympathy. Similarly, the poem can only demonstrate that it is itself and not the thing it describes (and this object may be internal as well as external) by comprehending it within itself, the result being the conviction of difference or novelty. If this is so, poetry can be seen as a repression of the object or, rather, of the objectivity of the object, which aims at involving the object without accepting it on its own terms. Perhaps it may even be said that, in its concern with giving the interest of novelty, poetry seeks to libidinize its object.

The question of the poem's identity-difference relation to its object brings to mind the question of synonymy raised by Coleridge's Second Aphorism. The fundamental significance of the Second Aphorism for Coleridge's larger purpose in *Biographia*

---

[1] M. H. Abrams, *The Mirror and the Lamp* (Oxford: Oxford University Press, 1953), p. 35.

is as an indication of the act of repression involved in the poet's insistence that this poem has always been as it is now. Similarly Coleridge's cardinal points indicate an incomplete repression—a pervasive fear really, that the poem can easily be replaced by the object it represents if it is not powerfully repressed. The poem must successfully repress the suspicion that it would simply be an irrelevance were it not for its success in removing the object itself from the scene of writing.

Returning for a moment to the Second Aphorism, we can see that what it *says* is that, in context of the poem, even synonyms are not equally intelligible. What Coleridge's cardinal points say is that the representation can comprehend its object by comprehending its meaning or, rather more accurately, by giving it meaning. But the repressed question is, of course: is the representation's intelligibility equal to that of the object? or, to put it slightly differently, is the representation a presence sufficient to fill the void left by the object's absence?

Perhaps the most revealing thing about this question is the violence we must do to the word "intelligibility" in order to ask it. Surely an object is not intelligible in the same sense as a representation. The intelligibility of the object refers to its distinct identity whereas the intelligibility of the representation refers to its meaning. In other words, the intelligibility of the representation is dependent upon the precedence of meaning over object. The intelligibility of the object is more a promise than an accomplished fact—a promise that is realized only insofar as we are prepared to treat objects as representations. Thus, the object may fancifully be conceived as a representation in search of a meaning. On the other hand, it is precisely the complacency of the object, the unassailability of its objective identity, which allows it to constitute the possibility of meaning without itself being meaningful. Paradoxically, meaning takes the self-evidence of the object as its ideal goal, even though the self-evident is necessarily meaningless. The object's promise of intelligibility is the result of its forceful impact on the senses. At the same time, the initiation of a movement toward meaning requires a resistance to the impact of the object. In his work on Wordsworth, Hartman has dealt extensively with the tyranny of the eye. Without sight, poetry is hardly imaginable, yet the very im-

138  pact of a visual impression threatens to swamp all attempts to develop it and realize it into a more complex awareness.[2]

As the first step in his attempt to define "poem" and "poetry" in the second half of *Biographia* XIV, Coleridge adopts the terms "pleasure" and "truth" to describe the immediate ends proper to poetic and scientific compositions (*BL*, II, 8–10). This first step in Coleridge's attempt at a "philosophical" definition corresponds closely to the first step in his account of the genesis of *Lyrical Ballads*, for "pleasure" and "truth" correspond to the two types of intelligibility that we have been discussing. Pleasure, in Coleridge's sense, is the anticipation of a realized intelligibility, and it is a faith in this potential intelligibility that elicits assent and cooperation in the present. This at least helps to clarify the relationship between pleasure as an immediate object and what Coleridge calls "poetic faith"—the "willing suspension of disbelief" (*BL*, II, 6). Truth, on the other hand, answers to a realized intelligibility which precedes its objects, or, rather, the immediate intelligibility guarantees the presence of its object instead of vice versa.

The full extent of the correspondence between Coleridge's account of *Lyrical Ballads* and his definition of a poem can only be comprehended if we go a step farther to the recognition that, whatever the priority assigned, both the poetic and scientific compositions seek not only to comprehend their objects within themselves but are themselves objects as well. In the case of the poem,

[2] Geoffrey H. Hartman, *Wordsworth's Poetry 1787–1814* (New Haven: Yale University Press, 1964), pp. 240–42. Less recent but quite interesting is Frederick A. Pottle's "The Eye and the Object in the Poetry of Wordsworth," in *Romanticism and Consciousness*, ed. Harold Bloom (New York: Norton, 1970), pp. 273–87. Michel Foucault argues in his essay "A Preface to Transgression," in *Language, Counter-Memory, Practice: Selected Essays and Interviews by Michel Foucault*, ed. Donald F. Bouchard (Ithaca: Cornell University Press, 1977), pp. 46–49, that if the power of sight threatens the disappearance of the subject, the act of closing the eye or rolling it upward into the skull is a transgression which reasserts the power of the subject. And in a lecture which would have interested Coleridge very much, Jacob Bronowski points out that modern research has revealed that we owe the precision of our sight (despite the physical crudity of the eye as an instrument) to the fact that we are apparently preprogrammed for the recognition of borders, of straight versus curved surfaces, and of other constitutive visual phenomena. Thus, our most fundamental sensory processes are actually based on active inference and not mere passive receptiveness (*The Origins of Knowledge and Imagination*, Silliman Memorial Lectures, 1967 [New Haven: Yale University Press, 1978], pp. 10–18).

where the presence of the object-as-representation is a guarantee of intelligibility, this is especially important. Coleridge's famous remark that "nothing can please which does not contain in itself the reason why it is so and not otherwise" (*BL*, II, 9), far from being a simple assertion of the self-defining nature of the poem, points, in part, to the poem's own objectivity as the source of its power to please. He develops this idea further by defining a poem as a composition "discriminated by proposing to itself such delight as is compatible with a distinct gratification from each component part" (*BL*, II, 10) and later by remarking of poetry that it has the "property of exciting a more continuous and equal attention than the language of prose" (*BL*, II, 11). In other words, poetry calls special attention to its parts, to the quality of its language, as a means of establishing that objectivity which guarantees the objectivity of the whole. Of course, as Coleridge himself points out, there is always the danger that the objectivity of the parts may swamp the intelligibility of the whole and immediate pleasure obscure ultimate truth.

Returning to Coleridge's account of *Lyrical Ballads*, we see that in his second cardinal point, the modifying colors of the imagination give the interest of novelty to poetry, which is to say that the imagination suffuses everything in the poem with its light (distorts in its own image might be more exact), and the result is not imagination measured by the standard of described reality but reality measured by imagination or, rather, reconstructed in its image. According to Coleridge, the practicability of combining both aspects of poetry (as outlined in the cardinal points) is represented by "the sudden charm which accidents of light and shade, which moonlight diffused over a known and familiar landscape. . ." —which is also not a bad illustration of the action of the "modifying colours" of the imagination. This, he tells us, is the "poetry of Nature" (*BL*, II, 5). The very objectivity of this example, the concreteness of its appeal to sensory experience, nearly seduces us into taking it at face value. But if it achieves nothing else, the philosophizing of Volume I at least prepares us to recognize this implicit distinction between the "truth" and the "poetry" of nature. The truth of nature is ultimately its absolute literality; the same landscape, whatever light falls upon it, and however much it is transformed, is always literally itself—there is no Proteus to bind together its myriad appearances into a single identity. The image serves to dissolve "nature," or at least this tiny bit of it, into the potentially infinite play of its manifestations, revealing the degree to which Wordsworth's nature is indeed poetic; which is to say that it is dependent on the same play of identity and difference that makes the poem possible.

Coleridge's second cardinal point indicates the presence of a hunger, presumably of the imagination, for a certain relation between the novel and the familiar—for the conviction of difference which opens up the world as a play of possible alternatives. The great obstacle to the satisfaction of this hunger is the "film of familiarity"—that deadening of apprehension which is the normal state of our relations with the world around and which poetry seeks to overcome (*BL*, II, 6). Paradoxically, this familiarity, which is in a very real sense an absence of awareness of the object, is the result of the object being present in all its literality. *For us*, the object only achieves full presence on its removal or repression. Leaving a trace of its former presence, a simulacrum of itself, it is most real to us in precisely that moment in which it is no longer itself but something else.[3] Novelty, far from being an attribute of the object, refers to this moment, at the center of Coleridge's understanding of poetry, when the film of familiarity—the implicit or immanent norm conditioning experience and masquerading as the real—is simultaneously revealed and removed. This moment comes about as the result of poetry's repression of the objectivity of the object in order to "re-present" it, wedded to the structure of its repression. There is at the beginning of the poetic process a coincidence of repressions: the poet represses in order to write, and the poem represses in order to be "about" something. As a result, the poem has some of the attributes of a genuinely human inwardness yet remains stubbornly distinct from the inwardness of the man who wrote it. For both poet and poem, the object comes to be defined by the peculiar shape of the self's or poem's repression of that objectivity. The object is, in a sense, pure presence—the pres-

[3] In this connection, Jacques Derrida's concept of the "trace" is valuable, even though I am not operating here within a strictly semiotic conceptual framework (*Of Grammatology*, trans. Gayatri Chakravorty Spivak [Baltimore: Johns Hopkins University Press, 1976], pp. 70–71).

ence that overwhelms. The problem faced in each poem is how to achieve presence without being trapped in the literality of the object. Coleridge's "familiarity," on the other hand, points to that implicit knowledge that simultaneously shields us from experiencing the world as a crazy-quilt of literal fragments, even as it threatens to make meaning the vehicle of our increased abstraction rather than of our enhanced reality. In this sense, poetry is concerned with making meaning itself once more meaningful.

On the basis of his cardinal points, Coleridge goes on to say that he and Wordsworth were led to speculate on the possibility of composing a collection of poems of two sorts: first, poems of the supernatural, the excellence of which would consist in the interesting of the affections by the dramatic truth of such emotions as would naturally accompany such situations if real; and second, poems of ordinary or everyday life, the subjects of which might be found wherever there is a meditative and feeling mind to seek after them (*BL*, II, 5). These may be briefly summarized as finding the normal in the novel and the novel in the normal. The nature of the second undertaking is clear enough: to penetrate the "film of familiarity" that deadens our awareness of everyday things. The poem of the supernatural, on the other hand, which was Coleridge's part of the *Lyrical Ballads* plan, is a good deal less straightforward in its nature and purpose.

The supernatural is not just a stretching or extension of the natural; it is created in some (presumably) negative relationship to nature through a consistent repression of whatever appears to be "natural." Thus, the first thing to appear in a poem of the supernatural is an extraordinarily strong presence of the normally implicit "nature." And because this nature is after all a construct, there also appears an equally strong presence of the inwardness that would manifest itself in this specific play of differences between natural and supernatural. In poems like "Kubla Khan" and "The Rime of the Ancient Mariner," Coleridge may be said to have adopted this principle in order to supernaturalize his own poetic procedure, exposing its inner workings (and, incidentally, revealing its inadequacy to deal with its own implications). Thus, Coleridge's supernatural serves as an important instance of the willed discontinuity which yields a definition of the undefined continuity. It also serves as Coleridge's most comprehensive paradigm of the special kind of presence that poetry bestows on consciousness and its objects— a presence distinct from all concepts of self or nature.

Coleridge remarks that he proposed to write poems of the supernatural so as to "transfer from our inward nature a human interest and semblance of truth sufficient to procure the willing suspension of disbelief which constitutes poetic faith" (BL, II, 6). This is, in a sense, a reader's-eye definition of the discontinuity involved in entering any text, brought into especially sharp relief by the special nature of the supernatural. As the form most frankly "transferred from our inward nature," most frankly determined to range itself against the natural, and giving the most emphasis to the reader's sense of having crossed over into another world, the supernatural emphasizes ultimately the power of the text alone to serve as the revisionary, corrective context of our "normal" experience of the world.

So far in our examination of Coleridge's account of *Lyrical Ballads*, we have overlooked one point: it argues the presence of an interpretation which preceded the poems. According to Coleridge, *Lyrical Ballads* was not (at least exclusively) the result of spontaneous overflowings of powerful feelings nor of emotions recollected in tranquillity; they proceeded from a plan which was, in turn, based on a sophisticated interpretation. In this sense, Coleridge's account undoes the poet's fiction that the origins of poems are poetic—that the poem finds and defines its own origin in its subject matter. This suggests that poems do not so much define their own origins as repress them in order that they may seize upon the act of repression (suitably disguised) as a point of origin. The fiction of poetic origins is that they are to be found in a special relationship between the poem and its subject matter and, therefore, between poetry and external nature. Coleridge's account of the genesis of *Lyrical Ballads* implies that the origin of poems is in the relationship between poetry and interpretation and that it is poetry's relation to knowledge (which constitutes "nature" in its own image and therefore constitutes the possibility of nature as we perceive it), not to nature, which is of prime importance.

There is still another important question to be asked about this account, for it appears to be at least conceivably another "I have always believed about poetry what I believe now" statement,

and we cannot help wondering if it is literally true or, like the
Second Aphorism, a folded-over admission of the original act of
forgetting, "my poem is and has always been" (that is, I have
merely recovered a poem which existed implicit in my subject
matter and in my mind when I first began to write).

But how can both of these interpretations of Coleridge's
account be right? The first seems to assume its literal truth, the
second to deny it. It is possible for both to be true because, for interpretation, truth is unimportant except as a matter of interest. Interpretation's concern is with intention, not truth or, more accurately, with that truth which can only be reached by means of the
notion of intention. Of course, some confusion is caused by the
failure to distinguish fact from truth. Even in a relatively straightforward autobiography, which *Biographia* definitely is not, the
inevitable inclusion of some facts to the exclusion of others is an
elementary act of figuration, which constitutes the possibility of a
corresponding interpretation. Or, rather, it constitutes that immanent intentionality which is the basis and the goal of interpretation,
which is to say that interpretation concerns itself with that which
refers to but cannot be contained within the notions of subject
and object. On the other hand, sometimes the intention is simply
to present a fact in its literality as sufficient to define its own intention (that is, intention appears to be irrelevant), in which case there
is no work for the interpreter. Insofar as a fact may be one from
among many, selected because it seems sufficient, it is an interpretation subject to further interpretation. And insofar as it both
represents and distorts the many in its own image, it is also an act
of figuration. Still, it is important to remember that even if no fact
is really self-sufficient, we nonetheless agree to treat certain facts
as if they were, not so much because of the inherent nature of the
fact but because of our conventionalized understanding of the intention behind it, manifested in the kind of composition in which
it appears.

The greater number of facts, like the "sky is blue," are
what a philosopher would call "true for some possible worlds,"
which is to say that it is possible to conceive of worlds in which
these statements are not true without logical absurdity. By contrast,
a statement like a "wife is a woman" or "a mother is a woman
with child or children" is "true for all possible worlds." Given

144 the intention to define one as the other, a world in which this is not the case is absurd. In this sense, it is intention which distinguishes fact from truth. Another thing that these observations make apparent is that a fact is a fact with reference to the "norm" of experience. In this respect, the "fact" is much like the "object" discussed earlier, for "fact" and "object" are not so much attributes of things or experiences in themselves so much as they are mental acts performed upon them.[4] Our own emotions are as susceptible to this "objectification" as things are. "Fact" objectifies with reference to a norm of experience, just as "object" objectifies with reference to a norm of concreteness provided by the physical object (which is to say that whatever the concreteness of the perceived object in itself, the senses are limited in their capacity to discriminate in the act of sensation). The similarity between the "fact" of interpretation and the "object" of poetry strongly suggests their interaction at the point of intention, "intention" being defined as "that world for which everything in a work is both true and sufficient" (for "world" we might well substitute some term such as the "intentional context" of phenomenology). Although this intentionality is primarily an attribute of the inwardness of poems, the coincidence between the acts of repression that make a poet and a poem possible determines that the "world for which everything in a work is both true and sufficient" is inhabited by "that being of whom everything in the work is equally an attribute"—the immanent author.

The question of intention also figures quite prominently in Coleridge's attempts at defining "poem" and "poetry." His analysis of the nature of the poem begins from the observation that the poem contains the same elements as a prose composition but in a different combination in consequence of a different object proposed (*BL*, II, 8). In the case of poetry, this is the immediate object of giving pleasure. Coleridge concludes that a poem is

[4] In a discussion of the general implications of Gödel's and Tarski's theorems, Bronowski argues that ". . . is true" is not a statement about any external object but about the statement itself. The inherent reflexiveness of the concept of truth (or of fact) immediately throws any construction into the realm of interpretation—even the most abstract mathematical language. Insofar as being an object and being conceived of as an object are clearly distinguishable, the same argument can be extended to include that concept as well (*The Origins of Knowledge and Imagination*, pp. 98–99).

that species of composition which is opposed to works of science by proposing for its immediate object pleasure, not truth; and from all other species (having this object in common) it is discriminated by proposing to itself such delight from the whole as is compatible with a distinct gratification from each component part. (*BL*, II, 10)

Coleridge elaborates his definition of a poem with this definition of a "legitimate poem" as "one the parts of which mutually explain and support each other; all in their proportion harmonizing with and supporting the known influences of metrical arrangement" (*BL*, II, 10).

Virtually everything that Coleridge says here about the poem is based on the observation that poetry excites a more continuous attention to its language than prose. We have already explicated much of this part of Chapter XIV, but one or two points of interest remain to be discussed. The first of these is that despite the apparently formalistic definition of the poem, Coleridge actually regards the difference between poetry and prose as one of almost pure intentionality. A man who intends to write a poem writes in a certain way because he intends to be understood in a certain way. The more or less formalistic elements of Coleridge's definitions indicate (primarily on the basis of their difference from the "nonpoetic" rather than of any defining similarity among themselves) the presence of an intention distinguishable from other intentions, but they are unable to define it. Coleridge's definition of a poem, involving a poetic experience which eludes it, offers the inadequacy of its own facticity as evidence that the concrete elements of poetic composition cannot define the truth of poetry—that meter, rhyme, and the harmony of the part with the whole (itself almost meaningless in the absence of an individual poem) are not sufficient indicators of poetic intentionality. In short, the formal elements of poetic composition do not comprise a "nature" within which and by whose laws a poet must work. These conventions are the tools of a poetic intentionality (which, as we concluded in Chapter 4, is equally inadequate to explain the enterprise of poetry) and function as its expressions; they are not the analogues of natural forms and natural laws. Thus, the poem emerges as a meaningful or intelligible utterance only within the context of the interpretive entity "poetry," in much the same way that an allegory finds its meaning or achieves intelligibility only within the context of the interpretive entity "symbol."

Coleridge's discussion of "poetry," which immediately follows, seems to exist largely to undo whatever faith we may have in his earlier definition of a poem. His formal definitions present us with the "facts" of a poem, but his discussion of poetry gives us the truth of the matter: poetry may exist without meter; Isaiah is undoubtedly poetry, yet it cannot be asserted that its immediate object is pleasure; and a poem of any length cannot and should not be all poetry, although some parts must be preserved in keeping with poetry by the property of exciting a more continuous and equal attention than the language of prose; but even this is not peculiar to poetry (*BL*, II, 11).

His definition of a poem, a test of the sufficiency of the accessible facts, was an attempt to define from the outside in, as it were. Undoing that definition, his discussion of poetry points to the need to define from the inside out. More important, the conflict between two modes of definition indicates a fundamental discontinuity between a "poem" and "poetry." The poem exists by virtue of its insistence on the priority of its object, for it is only that insistence which allows it to define its own origin. "Poetry," an apprehension of the totality of poems, understands at least implicitly that it constitutes the possibility of a poem as much, if not more, than the individual poem constitutes the possibility of poetry. Individual poems and poetry are much more nearly simultaneous creations than any individual poem can conceivably suggest. This is because both poem and poetry are equally unnatural—they originate in the same act of creation in which nature originates, and their relation to nature is a matter of convention, not of inherency. Like the New Dispensation, the simultaneity of creation saddles us with a freedom we do not want and hardly know what to do with. We read Genesis and point to the belatedness of man's creation, conveniently forgetting that in our belatedness we were the capstone of creation not its afterthought. Defining from the outside in (and here we have the motivation for Coleridge's attack on induction in "Essays on the Principles of Method"), we seek to evade the knowledge that intention constituted the possibility of all things and that we alone are capable of repeating that intention. The ostensible struggle of the poet, in individual poems at least, to free himself for the pure expression of self, the absolute achievement of his art, disguises even from himself the knowledge that he has carefully constructed his own dilemmas and that his poems exist as much to create perplexities as to resolve them.

More than anything else, *Biographia* XIV implicitly questions the idea that the distinctiveness of poetry depends upon the intensified presence either of the subject or the object. Like *Biographia* as a whole, the chapter functions (indeed, exists) through the continuous displacement of meaning: no sooner do we focus on the origin of *Lyrical Ballads* in search of the "truth" of poetry than the focus shifts to the impersonality and generality of "philosophical disquisition"; no sooner is a definition offered than another, emphasizing some different aspect of the poetic, is substituted; and no sooner do we begin to reconcile these multiple definitions than Coleridge points out that all of these defining characteristics also characterize works that are not really poems at all. Like the "nature" it describes, like the "author" or "poet" it implies, whatever it is that makes the poem poetic remains an immanence, eluding our grasp in the same moment we become aware of its presence. As has already been suggested in chapters 4 and 5, it is only when we consider the relationship among the poet, the poem, and nature at the encompassing level of poetry as an enterprise, of literature, and ultimately of the nature of the Bible, that the ceaseless play of figuration in which the poem represents the author, the author represents his poem, the poem represents nature, and so on, becomes more than a series of reductions, serving only to motivate still other unsatisfactory figures of an elusive truth.

Coleridge's difficulties in defining a "poem" further suggest that the problematical or indeterminate senses in which a poem is by someone, or about something, or even for someone are aspects of the even more encompassing problematic of "is": if it is not precisely any of these things or any combination of them, in what sense "is" the poem at all?

In the early chapters of his book *Freud and Philosophy,*

148 Paul Ricoeur distinguishes meaning from the consciousness or conviction of meaning, with regard to interpretation.[5] The consciousness is the conviction or sensation of meaning's presence whereas meaning gives definition to that presence but only at the cost of dispersing it among the referents of the phenomenal world (including the world of language which, though not completely phenomenal, is heavily implicated).[6] Ricoeur makes this distinction in the context of the much older recognition that identity and being are in fundamental conflict, since the former requires univocity of meaning and the latter cannot be univocally defined.[7] So another way to state our distinction between meaning and the consciousness of meaning is to say that the identity of meaning, manifested in the conviction of its presence, achieves definition by becoming conditional upon being—that is, by being dispersed among the various manifestations of being and represented by some of them.

From the point of view of interpretation, what the poem provides then is a meaning dispersed among or dissolved into particular manifestations of its being. I say "a meaning" because even though for poet and critic alike the act of writing begins with the conviction of meaning's presence, strictly speaking it has only theoretical existence as a meaning distinguishable from all other meanings until it has acquired the attributes implicit in its manifesta-

[5] In the introductory section of his book *Freud and Philosophy: An Essay on Interpretation*, trans. Denis Savage (New Haven: Yale University Press, 1970), pp. 3–56, Paul Ricoeur presents an impressively clear, concise examination of the relationships among symbol, reflection, and interpretation and details the fundamentally ethical conflict between what he calls a hermeneutics of postcritical faith (that is, of faith which has undergone examination) and a hermeneutics of suspicion, which operates on the assumption that consciousness is the encipherment of meaning. This distinction provides the terms necessary to define the confusions in Coleridge's theories of interpretation. Still working out of the biblical hermeneutic of faith, Coleridge's practical difficulties in making belief in the Word and belief in the critical/historical significance of the Bible one and the same reflect a subtle shift in the ambience of interpretation away from the faith that it will reveal the reality of correspondences to the suspicion that it may reveal irreducible disparity. Ricoeur's discussion of the relationship between the *Cogito Sum*, the conviction of meaning's presence, and reflection parallels from a philosophical point of view my own discussion of the significance of revision in defining the relationship between literature as a means of expression and literature as an instrument of knowledge.

[6] Ibid., pp. 43–45.

[7] Ibid., p. 23.

tions. Conditionally, the intention which is the goal of interpretation can therefore be seen as the identity of the meaning which is dispersed into the phenomenal world of the poem—its being.

But if the consciousness of meaning is without attributes until it has already been conditioned by being and dispersed among its manifestations, how is it that the consciousness of meaning is also a conviction of the identity of meaning? How is it that we can speak, however loosely, of "the" meaning of a poem or assume at least hypothetically that some interpretations are more representative of this meaning than others? The most immediate source of this conviction is the poem's identity as an object, with a distinct beginning and a distinct ending. The temptation is strong to say that the identity of the poem provides the basis for our conviction of the identity of its meaning, just as the identity of the natural object provides the basis for our conviction of the identity of subjective entities like ideas, feelings, even of experience itself. This is interesting because the identity of meaning undoubtedly does find its basis in the identity of objects. Unfortunately, it is by no means clear that the identity of objects is self-explanatory, which also means that it is by no means certain that the priority of the identity of objects over the identity of ideas is a matter of necessity and not convention or choice. Perhaps what poetry recognizes, even if the poet does not, is that there is no natural analogue of meaning.

Although the natural object preexists any description of it, the description must, nevertheless, condition and assume priority over the object if it is to have any comprehensible meaning. I wish to stand by my suggestion that the identity of the poem is of prime importance in promoting our conviction of the identity of the poem's meaning, even though it is becoming increasingly apparent that the objective existence of the poem is more problematical than might be supposed. What happens to this identity if, instead of being printed on its own page(s), set aside by a title, as is commonly done (indeed, so commonly that convention has made it an integral part of what is understood by the term "poem"), the poem is printed continuously with other poems or simply inserted in a much larger body of verse? How would the identity of the poem fare under such conditions?[8] The poem in its identity as object is dependent

[8] See Michel Foucault, "What Is an Author?" in *Language, Counter-Memory, Practice*, pp. 115–38.

150 on the identity of its meaning. If the identity of the poem is not self-evident either, or is not self-explanatory anyway, then there must be some principle prior to that of the identity of the object, which conditions both the subject and the object of the poem. This principle can be called that of the intentional object, and it refers us directly to biblical textuality as Coleridge defines it.

The failure of the poem to define sufficiently the grounds upon which meanings can function as objects and objects as meanings suggests that it is the nature of poetry to render both the subject and the object problematical and submit them to the test of indeterminacy. To disperse the conviction of meaning's identity or of the identity of the object into the phenomenal world of the poem or into the world of its subjective meanings is to provide the conditions under which the conviction of meaning, for example, can be contextualized. Perhaps it would be even more accurate to say that rather than placing the conviction of meaning in an experiential or phenomenal context that gives it substance, poetry reveals the conviction of meaning as the context in which experience and even phenomena exist. The way in which, under the pressure of scrutiny, poetic content and context continuously exchange roles indicates that the relationship between the conviction of meaning and its being in the world of the poem (or in the world, period) is not commutative—that is, once committed to poetic figuration, the conviction of meaning cannot be regained by a simple reversal. Meaning must be won back by means of an interpretation that is not the mirror image of figuration. The poem is not sufficient to determine or to circumscribe the interpretation proper to it because interpretation is not primarily determined by the existence of a specific object to interpret but by man's position in a world partly self-created and partly created by God. The distinction between the poem and the interpretation is a real one, but it defies all formal and all intentional definition; it exists only in relation to this ultimate condition and not by virtue of anything inherent in either the subject or the object of interpretation.

In order to clarify this somewhat, let us return for a moment to the term introduced in our discussion of *The Statesman's Manual*. For postbiblical man, the origin of an awareness of God is indistinguishable from the immanence of the revealed Word in the words of the Bible. Through the Bible (and the historical awareness that it initiated), we can see how God's original miraculous revelations of His presence initiated figuration as a movement toward the fullness of that immanent Being—a movement of which history itself is the profoundest expression. The Bible itself, as the continuing vehicle of this revelation—the text embodying its perpetual presentness—initiates interpretation as the mode of our self-conscious participation in the textual form of the revelation. Because of our position within the history initiated by the Bible, it is possible for poems (for example) to interpret and for interpretations to be poetic. But because the Bible distinguishes between itself and the origins it describes, because the Word is immanent in its words, and, ultimately, because God is "only" immanent in the world, figuration and interpretation remain distinct. Neither is reducible to the other; each is immanent in the other.

The play of identity and difference and the consequent displacements of meaning that mark our experience of Chapter XIV are brought to a conclusion (in *The Friend*, with a greater degree of self-awareness, Coleridge refers to such "conclusions" as "landing places") by still another famous definition of imagination. There is much significance, and no little irony, in the fact that Coleridge begins his remarks by asserting:

> What is poetry? is so nearly the same question with, what is a poet? that the answer to the one is involved in the solution to the other. For it is a distinction resulting from the poetic genius itself, which sustains and modifies the images, thoughts and emotions of the poet's own mind.
> (*BL*, II, 12)

Even if we fail to be alerted by the evasiveness of that "nearly," registering once again the point-counterpoint of identity and difference, the elusiveness throughout Chapter XIV of an answer to the question What is poetry? suggests not only that the nature of the poet is equally elusive but that it is elusive in very much the same way for the same reasons. The quality of being poetic, for man and poem, Coleridge suggests, is an immanence that resists abstraction.

According to Coleridge, what distinction there is between

152 the two questions is a product of the poetic genius itself, which sustains and modifies the images, thoughts, and emotions of the man. Presumably, what makes this genius poetic is the fact that it manifests itself in poetry; it becomes present in and is known through its poems. In this sense, poet and poetry are nearly the same: the qualities of the poetic genius immanent in the man are approachable only through the equally immanent poetry of the text.

Perhaps most striking, however, is the very problematical relationship between genius and self. That which we think of as the substance of consciousness—images, thoughts, and emotions— and thus the experiential basis for the conviction of self, is distinguished here from poetic genius. By implication, the poet as much as the reader can only reach out to that immanent poetic genius through the poetry. There is no shortcut through the self, for all the poet will find out from his images, thoughts, and emotions is what or where his poetic genius is not. Yet if the substance of poetic genius resides in the poems, the identity remains incomplete, first, because poetry—the quality of being poetic—remains immanent in the poems, and, second, and most importantly, because it requires a person to be a poet or to make a poem. Human inwardness and poetic inwardness, though they are similar enough to sustain a certain amount of confusion, are not finally the same any more (or any less) than God's immanence in the world and the immanence of the Word in the words of the Bible are the same. Because human and poetic inwardness are finally different, they sustain different immanences: the poet immanent in the poem remains different, though very like, the poet immanent in the man. Finally, the immanences—of poetry in poem, of poet in poem, of poet in self—that express and are aspects of our plight are not precisely interchangeable or analogous because immanence itself marks both the substance and limit of our existence in God's creation.

Here we approach, perhaps more closely than at any other point in this essay, the central problem confronting Coleridge in his critical, philosophical, and literary efforts: his belief in God commits him to the ultimate truth of the asymmetry between God as subject and man as subject in relation to the world. Man finds a place for himself in a world not of his own creation only through the mediation of the Bible and of the history and culture that it originates—there is no direct route through nature any more than through the self. "Immanence" refers to this asymmetry that places a conviction of difference at the heart of every identity and makes of every analogy a play of figures. Coleridge remarks very near the end of "Essays on the Principles of Method," perhaps his most sustained confrontation with the problem of immanence:

considered intellectually, individuality, as individuality, is only conceivable with and in the Universal and Infinite, neither before or after it. No transition is possible from one to the other, as from the architect to the house or the watch to its maker. The finite form can neither be laid hold of, nor is it anything of itself real, but merely an apprehension, a framework which the human imagination forms by its own limits, as the foot measures itself in the snow; and the sole truth of which we must again refer to the divine imagination, in virtue of its omniformity; even as thou art capable of beholding the transparent as little during the absence as during the presence of light, so canst thou perceive the finite things as actually existing neither with nor without the substance. Not without, for then the forms cease to be, and are lost in night. Not with it, for it is the light, the substance shining through it, which thou canst alone really see.
(EPM, 520)

If Coleridge must ultimately admit the figurative nature of any rational description of the individual's relationship with the world, he is, nonetheless, able to escape the limitations of philosophical idealism. Even though he makes extensive use of the vocabulary associated with that position to deconstruct the Wordsworthian faith in nature as a measure of the real, he argues finally the historical, rather than inherent, nature of the problem. The Bible's revelation of interpretation as a means of mediating between human understanding and God's truth is also a revelation that God's truth is ultimately beyond us. In effect, this revelation authorizes man to exercise fully his powers of rational understanding but only in the context of an understanding of their limits.

In Essay X of "Essays on the Principles of Method," Coleridge argues that it is part of man's "religious instinct" to view the phenomena of life, both within himself and in the world around, as "effects" with "causes" beyond themselves implying some end or purpose (EPM, 498–99). In the same chapter, Coleridge gives an account of the progressive "education" of man throughout history, beginning with the Hebrews and ending with modern Christianity (EPM, 500–506). In this account, he argues that men have not always sought a transcendent cause, that, instead, they once sought the causes of phenomena in other phenomena. The fact that in the ancient world almost every phenomenon of importance might have its own god reflects the degree to which meanings and objects were not only interchangeable but indistinguishable. Much of what is chronicled in the Old Testament deals with the conflict in the minds of men between a single transcendent God and a multitude of gods, trapped in the phenomenal world.

In Coleridge's view, the Bible gives voice to and therefore constitutes the possibility of the paradoxical notion of the intentional object, for the Bible establishes the conditions for the identity of being. Infusing the events of the Old Testament with God's manifest intentionality, the Bible establishes not nature but the text as the paradigm of the intentional object; natural objects are intentional objects only insofar as we view them as texts. Thus, it is through the Bible, which constitutes the notion of a text, that interpretation is able to appropriate the world to the ongoing enterprise, the pursuit of meaning.

The reasons for Coleridge's defense of miracle become even clearer in this connection, for the notions of the text and of the intentional object are only possible in the context of what is understood to be God's discontinuous and "unnatural" revelation in the Bible (thus, "natural" analogues of meaning are themselves fundamentally unnatural). Coleridge argued in *The Statesman's Manual* that eventually the identity of the miracle's meaning would replace its literal, objective identity (*SM*, 9–10). Ironically, the biblical revelation of the text is, by the same principle, superseded by the revelation as text. It is not only possible but inevitable that the continuing immanence of the text in history and culture not be limited by individuals' belief in God or even in the literal truth of Scripture.[9] This distinction is determined by the asymmetrical relationship between the text as God's revelation and the text as an instrument of human understanding. On the basis of the biblical revelation of the world as text, Coleridge asserts the priority of interpretation because, just as the revelation of the text must be replaced by the revelation as text, the poem as interpretation must be replaced by the interpretation of the poem (and perhaps even interpretation as poem). The best evidence that the text has indeed become the category conditioning experience is the increasing distinguishability of belief in meaning from belief in God or in the literal truth of Scripture. By the same token, the recognition that the natural analogue of meaning is only an analogue reflects the fact that the real analogues of meaning are now textual. In other words, the natural analogue of meaning is itself a mediate interpretation—a figuration of the text and hence an instance of the textualization of the world at the hands of interpretation.

In *Biographia* XIV, Coleridge says that "the poet, described in ideal perfection, brings the whole soul of man into activity, with the subordination of its faculties to each other according to their relative worth and dignity" (*BL*, II, 12). Looking back to Coleridge's earlier definition of a "legitimate poem" (one "the parts of which mutually explain and support each other; all in their proportion harmonizing with and supporting the purpose and known influences of metrical arrangement"), we can see that Coleridge comes as close as possible, without confusing people and poems, to arguing that the internal qualities of good poets and good poems are one and the same. And since it is imagination that makes this harmony of elements possible, he offers it as much as a quality of poems as of poets. To put it another way, imagination serves to name that immanent inwardness that poets and poems can and do share. But as the subsequent definition shows, not even imagination (especially not imagination) escapes the limits imposed on articulation by immanence.

[9] This progressive disassociation of the notion of the text and the work of interpretation from a belief in God or the literal truth of Scripture is the subject of Hans W. Frei's *The Eclipse of Biblical Narrative: A Study in Eighteenth- and Nineteenth-Century Hermeneutics* (New Haven: Yale University Press, 1974).

In order to approach the notion of poetic genius and, through it, of imagination, Coleridge distributes rhetorically the unarticulated conviction of self into discrete qualities or manifestations, reified as "faculties." The creation of "faculties" out of the fleeting phenomena of the mind is a process of distillation that leaves behind a theoretical self, defined almost totally in terms of what it is not, which preserves the tenuous link between faculties and the immediate, if unarticulated, evidence of consciousness. If this diaspora demonstrates the degree to which the solidity of the conviction of self depends on its unarticulated nature, it also emphasizes the potential incompatibility between the identity of the self and what it does (that is, articulating, distinguishing, cataloguing the world into an experience, unified by a single, unique referend, "me"). Thus, it is by creating an absence of self that Coleridge is able to posit imagination as that which unifies the discrete faculties into "self." Imagination then is distinguished from the faculties which it unifies and coordinates by the fact that it is not "discovered" by the reflexive examination of the materials so much as created by reflection itself. The incompatibility between a substantial sense of self as a presence and "imagination" is self-created. Thus, the analogues of imagination are natural only at the ultimate level of God's withdrawal from the created world in order to create a distinction between his identity and his manifestation, which is necessary if any experience is to pertain to man instead of directly to God.

God's self-abnegation creates the space within which human choice and human will achieve independence. Similarly, Coleridge's approach to imagination creates the space in which acts of will are known and identified, the space in which roads taken coexist with roads not taken. The substance of the self is in choices made, acts performed; yet the distinctness of the self depends on a knowledge of choices rejected, acts refrained from.

All of this points to one essential fact about Coleridge's enterprise in defining imagination: it is itself a sign of consciousness' search for literalization or embodiment for those elements in itself that seem uniquely human, antithetical to nature. Coleridge is seeking to avoid the inherent tension identified by Hartman in the poetry of Wordsworth between uniquely human powers and the need to embody them in images or forms drawn from nature.

According to the Coleridge of "Kubla Khan," the demonic or inhuman aspects of imagination are directly linked to the mis-conceived attempt to humanize it by limiting it within the realm of natural representation. This search for unnatural analogues leads in two directions: toward the textual model of the Bible and toward language, both of which possibilities are considered in Volume II of *Biographia*.

Coleridge goes on to describe the "power" of imagina-tion, which manifests itself in a "tone and spirit of unity that blends and (as it were) fuses, each into each . . ." (*BL*, II, 12). Coleridge's reference to the "power" of imagination is misleading since it represents an attempt to fix and define an event within the self whose own existence is posited from the traces it leaves on the page or in the poet's mind. The evidences of imagination are found in the self-initiated act, which is, in part, an attempt to articulate imagination. Imagination is both self-initiating and self-referential; and the first imaginative act is to assert the absence of imagination and the necessity to seek it out.

Coleridge's difficulty in describing imagination is an in-dication of the fact that he is dealing with an event initiated in language but which cannot be contained within that language. Or imagination is the necessary consequence of treating the self as a text. Consider this famous passage:

> This power, first put in action by the will and understand-ing and retained under their irremissive, though gentle and unnoticed control (laxis effertur habenis) reveals it-self in the balance or reconciliation of opposite or discord-ant qualities: of sameness with difference; of the general with the concrete; the idea with the image; of the indi-vidual with the representative; the sense of novelty and freshness, with old and familiar objects; a more than usual state of emotion, with more than usual order; judge-ment ever-awake and steady self-possession, with enthusi-asm and feeling profound and vehement; and while it blends and harmonizes the natural and the artificial, still subordinates art to nature; the manner to the matter; and our admiration of the poet to our sympathy with the poetry. (*BL*, II, 12)

As description, this passage raises a number of questions. In what sense can an act of will be unnoticed? Does the concept of balance really balance that of opposite? How is it that qualities defined as discordant become reconciled without becoming meaningless? The challenge of defining imagination, the effort of denoting and literalizing the primal act of figuration, seems to defeat language, setting its signifying and symbolizing functions against one another and revealing the potential antithesis of definition and meaning. Definition is the act initiating a movement toward meaning, but achieved meaning stands in contradistinction to mere definition (as connotation to denotation).

The whole passage creates the sensation of meaning by dissolving the identities of its terms, by dissolving their specific meanings. These particular meanings or definitions assure us that differences between the physical appearances of words are also differences in meaning. Given the idea of meaning and the physical differences between words, it is easy enough to recognize that words have different meanings by virtue of their different physical appearances, but beyond this is the recognition that meanings differ (and sometimes are alike) in ways unrelated to their physical incarnations. In the first instance, the physicality of words lends substance to the idea of differences in meaning, but it is the power of meanings to differ from each other in different ways (unlike words themselves which always differ in the same physical ways, hence grammar) which legitimizes the whole enterprise of incarnating meanings in words. Without words to give substance to the idea of meaning itself, this further distinction, belated as it is, would not be possible, but without it distinction in meaning would not be separable from distinction in appearance, and the whole enterprise of language would merely be redundant of experience.[10] What Coleridge does in this passage is to dissolve the identity of the meanings of his words (definitions) in order to ex-

[10] The effectiveness of Coleridge's rhetoric here is dependent upon a fundamental discontinuity between the power of the same word or phrase to function as a univocal or a plurivocal expression within the semantic field. Coleridge appears to achieve his definition of imagination by setting the signifying and symbolizing functions of language against one another. Thus, it would seem that the ground between signification and symbolization, in which both are active and neither rules, is the common domain of power of imagination and the activity of interpretation (Ricoeur, *Freud and Philosophy*, pp. 11–12).

ploit our basic recognition of the *fact* of their differing meanings. From a sufficiently literal viewpoint, his language is absurd, but it would be more accurate to consider his statement "deeply sense-less" because in distinguishing definition from meaning, it also distinguishes an accumulation of words from a language. What begins as an attempt to *define* imagination ends as a description of the difference between definition and meaning. Definition ini-tiates a movement toward meaning which is never completed. The accumulation of "balanced" contraries, each standing in a figurative relation to the others, is potentially infinite, brought to an arbitrary end only by the introduction of Davies' lines on the soul, which bring us back once again to immanence as the ulti-mate form of our difficulty in articulating the grounds upon which meaning can be seen as something achieved rather than as a con-tinuous process of displacement, indistinguishable from our his-torical and cultural existence (one is reminded here of the in-ternecine medieval squabbles over where in the body the soul resides).

As I have already suggested, the driving force here is the interpretation which isolates and defines faculties in the im-mediate phenomena of consciousness and which creates a by no means self-evident series of oppositions. In this context, something rather startling about "imagination" becomes clear: imagination is the self-image that the textualizing consciousness "discovers" in its object; it is the pretext which is the warrant for the textuali-zation performed by interpretation.

The textualization of consciousness which occurs here consists in the transformation of the phenomena of consciousness into "faculties." In other words, it involves imposing a vocabu-lary, a language, on its object. The concept of faculties is very interesting in itself since it would seem to attribute to the phe-nomena of consciousness many of the qualities of words, especially nouns and verbs, without bestowing the status of a language. This is the function attributed to imagination: the conversion of the "words" of consciousness (its utterances anyway) into a language (Coleridge would present it as the power which welds discrete sensations, emotions, and thoughts into consciousness). But the real nature of the textualizing consciousness becomes clear in the passage on "the balance or reconciliation of opposite or discordant

160   qualities," in which the skewed relationship between the definitions of the terms and the way in which they are used suggests
that what defines the text is the imposition of a language on a
language (that is, the imposition of one system of meanings on
another), and where textualizing consciousness finds no language,
it must create one as an attribute of its object.

If we turn from the task of defining imagination to the
example of the Bible, we can see how it imposes the language of
Christianity on the history and customs of the Ancient Hebrews.
It does this by creating a vocabulary of paganism to which it op-
poses itself and which it eventually incorporates. Beyond its illus-
trative value, the importance of the Bible in this connection clearly
has to do with Coleridge's desire, through the use of the concept
of imagination, to disengage the notion of the text from the notion of language or, rather, to distinguish the origin of the text
from the origin of language. As we have seen, Coleridge was in
fundamental agreement with the thinkers of his time about the
origin of language in primitive man's relation with nature. For
him, however, it did not follow that all the complex forms of modern language can be seen as continuous extensions of that origin
in nature. Coleridge saw clearly the difficulty of accounting (in
terms of a single theoretical origin) for language both as consciousness' way of imposing its forms on the external world and
as a way in which man is adapted to his environment by being
conditioned to its requirements. The way to avoid this dilemma
is to argue that the necessity of the idea of text is not inherent in
the idea of language. This is, in effect, to argue that that original
language was not language in the modern sense of the term. What
we know as language is the confluence of simple language as a
response to our human and natural environment and the development of the text, which is language's self-conscious recognition
that it is its own environment. The continuous refinement of the
text is a continuous refinement or reconditioning of the simple
language which is its primary tool.

Interpretation can be seen as a refinement in our conception of the text—a refinement which liberated new possibilities
in poetry, in part, as a pretext for its own development—and
imagination can be seen as one of interpretation's most important
pretexts and its most compelling self-image for the Romantic Age.

# 7

## THE ORDER OF NATURE
## AND THE ORDER OF THE TEXT:

### *Biographia* XVII and "Essays on the
### Principles of Method"

In *Biographia* XVII, Coleridge identifies the definitive instance of the integral relationship of consciousness and textuality through his celebrated attack on Wordsworth's theory of poetic diction—an attack which also brings him back to the subject of the Bible. The focal point of Coleridge's critique is the proposition that "the proper diction for poetry in general consists altogether in a language taken, with due exceptions, from the mouths of men in real life, a language which actually constitutes the natural conversation of men under the influence of natural feelings" (*BL*, II, 29). According to Wordsworth, this natural language exists in its purest form among scenes of low and rustic life

> because in that condition the essential passions of the heart find a better soil in which they can attain their maturity, are less under restraint, and speak a plainer and more emphatic language; because in that condition of life our elementary feelings coexist in a state of greater simplicity and consequently may be more accurately contemplated and more forcibly communicated; because the manners of rural life germinate from these elementary feelings, and from the necessary character of rural occupations are more easily comprehended and more durable; and lastly, because in that condition the passions of

men are incorporated with the beautiful and permanent forms of nature. (*BL*, II, 30–31)

We are not concerned here with determining whether, in quoting this passage, Coleridge is representing fairly Wordsworth's theory of poetry. Coleridge's choice does reflect his clear understanding that although other ideas may be more central to the Wordsworthian poetic, this implicit opposition of natural to literary language is the primary vehicle of Wordsworth's poetic ideology. Wordsworth's remarks involve a series of implicit assumptions, the most important of which is that since language itself originates in the relation of man to nature, the conversation of rustics expresses the clearest relation between the passions excited by the "beautiful forms of nature" and language. Such an assumption argues that man's relationship to nature is privileged; and it reduces a self-conscious literary language to the status of an accretion, implying that literature is an extension of an essentially responsive natural language.

But Wordsworth's argument takes a rather curious shape, for, in the final analysis, the priority of man's relationship with nature does not authorize natural language so much as the reverse: the superior *literary* qualities of what Wordsworth chooses to regard as natural language authorize the priority of the natural relationship. The language of Wordsworth's rustics is a response to the passions they feel in confronting nature, not a response to nature itself. This suggests that the linguistic response to nature (the fact that a response is called for and that it takes the form of language) is a defense against its overwhelming reality and that language quickly establishes itself in antithesis to those experiences which motivate it.

This uncertainty over the real function of natural language points to the begged question of "natural forms." The primary distinction between natural and literary language is clearly the latter's dependence on the model of the text—a difference that Wordsworth ignores. But we are more than justified in wondering whether the form of the text finds its origin in natural forms or in a language thoroughly conditioned by the model of the text, which imposes its own textuality on nature.

This is precisely the line of attack chosen by Coleridge when he remarks that the clear and immediate apprehension that Wordsworth sees in the language of the farmers and shepherds of Cumberland and Westmoreland is above all the result of the "solid and religious education which has rendered few books familiar but the Bible and the liturgy or hymn book." He goes on to say:

> To this latter cause indeed, which is so far accidental that it is the blessing of particular countries and a particular age, not the product of particular places or employments, the poet owes the show of probability that his personages really feel, think and talk with any tolerable resemblance to his representation. It is an excellent remark of Dr. Henry More's, that "a man of confined education, but of good parts, by constant reading of the bible, will naturally form a more winning and commanding rhetoric than those that are learned, the intermixture of tongues and of artificial phrases debasing their style." (*BL*, II, 31)

Those rustic qualities most admired by Wordsworth are the result not of the immediacy of nature but of the fact that their language is conditioned by a single textual model. Through language, the coherence of the biblical text is imposed on their experience of nature, and thus the model of the text is the basis for the conviction of natural form. Endorsing Dr. More's contrast between the unity and power of a single textual model and the confusion induced by a multitude of competing texts, Coleridge locates the reasons for the declining authority of the traditional canon not in any inherent weakness of literary language but in the multiplication of texts competing for authority and able to achieve it only at one another's expense. In suggesting that Wordsworth is actually referring to "the blessing of particular countries in a particular age," Coleridge throws the entire dispute into the realm of historical contingency, depriving Wordsworth of the a priori judgments on which his argument is based and revealing one of its greatest weaknesses: its inability to provide any sensible account of the historical development of language which is also

*164*   true to the complexity and diversity of modern language use.

Coleridge concludes with an attack on Wordsworth's notion that natural language is the authoritative source of modern discourse:

> The best part of human language, properly so called, is derived from reflections on the acts of the mind itself. It is formed by a voluntary appropriation of fixed symbols to internal acts, to processes and results of imagination, the greater part of which have no place in the consciouness of uneducated man; though in civilized society, by imitation and passive remembrance of what they hear from their religious instructors and other superiors, the most uneducated share in the harvest which they neither sowed nor reaped. If the history of the phrases in hourly currency among our peasants are traced, a person not previously aware of the fact would be surprized at finding so large a number which three or four centuries ago were the exclusive property of the universities and schools, and at the commencement of the Reformation had been transferred from the school to the pulpit, and thus gradually passed into common life. The extreme difficulty, and often the impossibility of finding words for the simplest moral and intellectual processes has proved perhaps the weightiest obstacle to the progress of our more zealous and adroit missionaries. (*BL*, II, 39–40)

Coleridge distinguishes between a truly primitive language of nature and a language growing out of inner reflection, associated with the need to articulate consciousness' self-experience. For Coleridge, the development of this inward language by the appropriation of fixed symbols to internal acts is also the process by which consciousness, a distinctly human inwardness, comes into being. A language tied too closely to nature holds man back from full humanity. And in that final sentence, Coleridge hints at the new revelation of biblical textuality, going on even now, which will put the unfortunate possessors of a genuinely natural language in full possession of their own human identities. Seeking to impose the language of inwardness on a natural language

of external limitation, the missionaries are helping their charges
to reenact our own simultaneous growth into textuality and self-
awareness.

The image of missionaries attempting to impose a religion based on the text of the Bible suggests that we look for the
origins of complex language in the confluence of religious impulse
and textuality. As Coleridge's account of the Hebrews in "Essays
on the Principles of Method" implies, it is the introduction of
biblical textuality that allows religion to condition our experience
of nature and not vice versa. In this context, what the Old Testament recounts is the development of textualizing consciousness as
the Hebrews learn to impose the abstract language of belief on
their own natural language, conditioned by the existence of no-
madic shepherds. The Bible both chronicles and embodies this
transformation, just as monotheism (as opposed to a polytheistic
nature worship) is both its cause and consequence.

In Essay X of "Essays on the Principles of Method," Coleridge offers a history of mankind's progressive "education," in
which he attempts to define the precise nature of the change
which occurred in our ways of perceiving in the time of the Old
Testament Hebrews. The central lesson learned by the Hebrews
according to Paul was that "through faith we understand that the
worlds were framed by the word of God; so that things which
were seen were not made of things which do appear." This para-
phrase of Hebrews 13:3 is interpreted by Coleridge: "The solution
of Phaenomena can never be derived from Phaenomena."

> Upon this ground [Coleridge tells us] the writer of the
> epistle to the Hebrews is not less philosophical than elo-
> quent. The aim, the method throughout was, in the first
> place to awaken, to cultivate, and to mature the truly
> human in human nature, in and through itself, or as
> independently as possible of the notices derived from the
> sense, and of the motives that had reference to the sensa-
> tions; till the time should arrive when the senses themselves
> might be allowed to present symbols and attestations of
> truths, learnt previously from deeper and inner sources.
> Thus the first period of the education of our race was
> evidently assigned to the cultivation of humanity itself;

or of that in man, which of all known embodied creatures he possesses, the pure reason as designed to regulate the will. (EPM, 500–501)

Coleridge's concern is to account theoretically and historically for the development of our power to *create* the world we perceive out of a more primitive language/consciousness, totally dominated by the paradigm provided by the phenomenal world. Implicitly, Coleridge's is an argument which sees men emancipating themselves from the authority of the natural paradigm by generating out of themselves an even more compelling symbolic and linguistic reality.

The first step in achieving this was the exciting in the Hebrews of "the idea of their Creator as a spirit, of an *idea* which they were strictly forbidden to realize to themselves under any *image*; and secondly, by the injunction of obedience to the will of a super-sensual Being" (EPM, 501). This first injunction was necessary in order to prevent the immediate reappropriation of God to the phenomenal world. As an extension of this desensualization, the rewards of obedience were placed at a distance. In contrast to the Hebrews were the biblical peoples who "determined to shape their convictions and deduce their knowledge from without, by exclusive observation of outward and sensible things as the only realities" (EPM, 501). According to Coleridge, the consequences of such a dependence on natural analogy are the true subject of the story of the Tower of Babel:

the men of sense, of the patriarchal times, neglecting reason and having rejected faith, adopted what the facts seemed to involve and the most obvious analogies to suggest. They acknowledged a whole bee-hive of natural Gods; but while they were employed in building a temple consecrated to the material Heavens, it pleased divine wisdom to send on them a confusion of lip, accompanied with the usual embitterment of controversy, where all parties are in the wrong, and the grounds of quarrel are equally plausible on all sides. As the modes of error are endless, the hundred forms of Polytheism had each its 167 group of partizans who, hostile or alienated, henceforward formed separate tribes kept aloof from each other by their ambitious leaders. Hence arose, in the course of a few centuries, the diversity of languages, which has sometimes been confounded with the miraculous event that was indeed its first and principal, though remote, cause. (EPM, 502–03)

These patriarchal men of sense were blind allegorizers—blind in the sense that they set about allegorizing a creation only partially apprehended. And in accepting the sufficiency of the sensible, they also accepted its fragmentation as their principle of limitation. By contrast, the Hebrews of the Old Testament learned not to seek final causes in the phenomenal world. Turning their attention from the diversity of nature (implying a polytheistic world), the Hebrews accepted a single spiritual deity, who defined himself in antithesis to nature by his unexpected, often miraculous interventions. What the Hebrews understood of this God was his law—the absolute power and harsh retribution. Mysterious beyond comprehension, their God brought them to see the inadequacy of all previous ways of seeing.

That God has a method, however incomprehensible his acts may seem, and that man's fate is bound up in this method are the messages of the Bible. In Coleridge's view, method itself begins with the Bible, for in its example is found our first authorization to attribute method and not just to obey. This generative text is, therefore, the origin of mind as we conceive it because the attribution of method is at once the salient characteristic of consciousness and textuality. And so the experience of the biblical text, and the assumption of method that we bring to it, provides the paradigm for the experience of the world as an order, and not vice versa.

Because the Bible is the manifestation of the Word, of God's method in history, it creates method as an attribute of the historical world—it no longer resides only in the mind of God (a distinction corresponding with that between the personal intentions of the author and the intentionality manifest in his text).

*168* When Coleridge argues that part of God's educative method was to show the Hebrews the inadequacy of the phenomenal world as the ground of reason, he is pointing out that this knowledge is not the result of a direct understanding of that time in history but is mediated by the Bible itself, by textualization. The Bible thus becomes the origin of history, and, in a very real sense, the history of the Old Testament Hebrews begins not with the fact of their existence but in the Bible. The way in which the Bible gives us entry into the world of the patriarchs is a figure for the way in which the model of the text gives us entry into all aspects of the postbiblical world. In this context, the text can be seen as what happens to language when man achieves historical consciousness —an awareness of identity in time.

As a group, "Essays on the Principles of Method" address themselves to the more modern Babel of competing discourses, of rival ways of textualizing the world. They are largely a dialogue between the Bible and modern philosophy, as it is represented by Hume's problem (that is, that no accumulation of empirical observation is ever sufficient to prove that something will happen). Identifying the true origin of Hume's problem in the lesson learned by the Old Testament Hebrews (to distrust phenomena as the basis of knowledge), Coleridge contrives to suggest that as a *problem*, it addresses itself less to the final nature of the world and status of knowledge than to the historical origins of our culture, which gave to consciousness its basically textual shape. In this way, Coleridge demonstrates the Bible's continued capability of assimilating to itself more recent forms of discourse (which it makes historically possible), including those which pretend to address themselves if not to last things then to ultimate problems.

Despite his agreement with Hume about the limits of induction,[1] Coleridge rejects the pretensions of his discourse because it is insufficiently aware of our plight as men. Knowledge cannot be sufficiently defined by its relation to logical verification any more than by its relation to simple faith. Truth and belief in the good are implicated in one another, and both are bound up in a textuality with its roots in biblical revelation. At the end of his

---

[1] Essay VI of "Essays on the Principles of Method" (I, 464–71) is concerned primarily with a critique of the limits of induction.

"Maranatha" essay, Walter Ong asks whether revelation came before or after textuality.[2] Coleridge would very likely have answered that they are one and the same.

Coleridge's response to contemporary philosophy's implicit opposition between standards of truth and goodness is suggested by the diversity of materials that he brings to bear on the problem raised by Hume: Shakespeare, Plato, Bacon, anecdote, history, the Bible, comparative religion, and so on. Method's relationship, both to the true and to the good, is confirmed by its success as a theme capable of relating and rendering comprehensible the diversity of cultural artifacts which make up an environment at least as "natural" to us as the phenomenal world. In its special relationship with Scripture, with science, and with personal experience, method represents the point at which a Shakespeare's or a Plato's concerns with the good and the true are seen to intersect. The immanence of method is both an a priori conviction and an authorization to interpret as a means of making that conviction true.

We began by defining revision as the concept linking the poet as creator to the poet as reader—a link made necessary for Coleridge by the increasing alienation that he felt from his own poetry. Coleridge generalized and objectified his personal alienation by arguing that the rise of a mass reading public, the power of the reviews, and the hubris of science and philosophy had combined to transform the social and intellectual context of literature and to embarrass the old literary/interpretive order, in which an accepted canon of ancient and modern works provided the basis for a generalized poetic diction. In such a situation, the poet could not help being more and more aware of the independence of the achieved poetic object in comparison with the poem-coming-into-being, still the exclusive possession of the poet's creative will. Thus, the concept of revision defines not only Coleridge's personal need to reappropriate to himself poetic utterances manifesting an intentionality that he is reluctant to acknowledge but also a general need to redefine poetry in order to reappropriate poems to some concept of literary order.

2 Walter Ong, *Interfaces of the Word: Studies in the Evolution of Consciousness and Culture* (Ithaca: Cornell University Press, 1977), p. 270.

We also defined the terms upon which the Bible provides the category (text) by which the disruptive forces of historical and natural contingency are subdued. The Bible appropriates all contingencies because it constitutes the comprehensive contingent disruption of an unreflective state of nature which defines the possibility of history as opposed to event, text as opposed to utterance, and method as opposed to fiat. As the paradigm of the text, the Bible makes language self-conscious, which is to say that from the inception of biblical textuality, language becomes reflexive and, hence, revisionary. As Coleridge defines it, biblical textuality, through the vehicle of language, makes history, science, and philosophy possible by imposing the self-referential structure of the text on events and phenomena.

Ironically, Coleridge's very success in discerning the shaping influence of the Bible immanent in the problematics of even the most "purely" philosophical and scientific pursuits presents him with a problem. For if the Bible constitutes the very shape of our existence, if the march of biblical history snatches away and appropriates to itself our acts as they are being performed, even our thoughts as they are being thought, where is the urgency of faith? What difference does the testimony—the acquiescence or apostasy—of the individual make? In this context, the distinction between human and textual inwardness—that same distinction which allows the contingent to intervene so disruptively in the poems—assumes not only a special importance but a positive aspect.

For one thing, this distinction, so troubling in its immediate implications for Coleridge the poet, establishes the space within which all those texts that are not the Bible and all those forms of knowledge not overtly religious find their legitimate functions. They are needed because the Bible itself does not finally transcend or stand apart from the history that it makes possible—after all, even in the Bible biblical history is presented as already begun. Among other things, this means that the Bible itself is not sufficient to define the hermeneutic proper to it. Even the Bible, properly understood, must be subordinated, however slightly, even subliminally, to a more general hermeneutic in which the goal of interpretation is to establish the terms on which *any* interpretive object is seen as a text in need of revision; whether by actually changing the language, by placing it in a new context, or by translation, it must be treated as something demanding our participation in order to achieve its fullest existence. In this way, revisionary interpretation becomes the means by which the individual inserts his distinctiveness into and achieves a sense of his active participation in the process of which he is already a part. In this way, interpretation itself is both a recognition of the true mediacy of our existence and a primary, active expression of faith. Each act of interpretation avoids the dismal alternative of faith established by the abridgement of reason by means of a saving of faith through reason. Thus, in Coleridge's view faith becomes the only utterly reasonable thing.

Coleridge's understanding that the Bible itself requires such a redemption by revision is reflected in his interest in the mythological school of the Higher Criticism. Placing the Bible itself within the context of revisionary interpretation, Coleridge and other mythological apologists subordinated the literal word of the biblical text to a broader understanding of its context as a means of appropriating the Bible to the state of contemporary knowledge.

During the latter half of the eighteenth century, rationalism and a strong interest in Oriental history and culture had combined to undermine the uniqueness of biblical revelation by showing that many of the stories and motifs of the Bible were also the property of Oriental culture rather than exclusively Judaeo-Christian. The most militantly rational of the Bible's eighteenth-century critics concluded from all this that the Bible was merely another myth, which should be treated in a completely secular context. In response, there grew up in Germany, aided by the sophisticated work of English Orientalists, a school of biblical apologists whose defense of the Bible was based on a revisionary elevation of myth from the status of priestly illusion to a language of universal human experience—in effect, a shared order of the self. These apologists saw in the Bible the synthesis and highest expression of that fundamental religious impulse and shared self-experience which was imperfectly articulated in the many myths composing the diverse religions of the Orient. In their view, the Middle East was the point at which all these tra-

*172* ditions met and mingled, and out of this encounter rose their synthesis in the Christian religion.[3]

Coleridge's own highly sophisticated involvement in this movement is evidenced in his concern with distinguishing the uniqueness of the Bible from its specialness in the opening pages of *The Statesman's Manual*.[4] By shifting the locus of the Bible's value, this distinction saves its authority from being compromised by the evidence that its contents are not unique, even as it solicits not mere acquiescence in the word but insight and active understanding of its qualities as the measure of our faith. And instead of taking the external evidence of the Bible's uniqueness as the confirmation of its value, Coleridge appeals to the internal evidence, confirmed in the individual's experience, as individual, of his own inadequacy, of the Bible's special relationship to a common way of experiencing the world and a shared religious impulse. In effect, to recognize the specialness of the Bible is also a self-recognition and a self-revision, acknowledging and participating in an immanent humanity—a humanity that is at once an aspect of self and the ground of our collective existence.

More specifically, and this too is the business of the "Method" essays, when immanence comes to be perceived not as uniquely characteristic of the Bible, nor even as a primarily re-

---

[3] For a more complete account of the mythological school and of Coleridge's involvement, see chapters 1–4 of E. S. Shaffer's *"Kubla Khan" and The Fall of Jerusalem* (Cambridge: Cambridge University Press, 1975). Herder's work on myth gave early impetus to the mythological movement through its influence on Eichhorn (who coined the term "Higher Criticism") and his pupil, Gabler. Coleridge read Eichhorn with great care, and, as J. Robert Barth has pointed out, the German was probably the single greatest source in Coleridge's exegetical background (*Coleridge and Christian Doctrine* [Cambridge: Harvard University Press, 1969], p. 56n.).

[4] This distinction is also made significant by its usefulness in clarifying the analogous distinction between priority or firstness and origin. To assume the equality of priority with origin is, in fact, an act of figuration, just as Coleridge argues that the equating of biblical uniqueness with the quality of its specialness is an act of figuration. The deemphasizing of biblical uniqueness in favor of specialness was necessary both to save the Bible from the implications of the Higher Criticism's critique of biblical uniqueness and to generalize the scriptural paradigm into other fields of endeavor, including literature. Shaffer notes that "The orthodox belief in the uniqueness of the Scriptures and their 'inspiration' by God was substantially undermined by treating the Books of the Bible as examples of Oriental Literature" (*"Kubla Khan" and The Fall of Jerusalem*, p. 21).

ligious concept but as equally characteristic of every aspect of the history and culture made possible by the Bible, then the Bible itself is appropriated to the process that it initiates; it truly does become *our* gift from God and the measure of our uniquely human gifts—a mediation standing for and participating in the mediacy of our existence.

This mediation encodes a relationship between knowledge and that qualitative experience of our own existence which we most urgently demand and need or between that aspect of existence which we possess and that which we most urgently desire. For mythological criticism, the Bible enunciates a relationship between the most complete knowledge of man's historical destiny and that destiny most to be desired. Within the Christian myth defined by this relationship, it is perpetually possible for the individual to experience his own existence in the most profound possible way, in the context of any historical moment. The quality of this experience is the sensation of participating in the totality of God's creation, not in spite of one's human and historical identity but because of it. In this way, Coleridge surrenders the literality of biblical revelation in order to save through an act of interpretation what it regards as its essential value.

From Coleridge's point of view, faith reveals itself most strongly, both as a personal attribute and as a necessary condition of existence, in that moment when it appears and then disappears back into the substance of what is known. The narrow assertion of faith as an attribute of the distinct self is not at all the same as the recognition that an individual's faith is immanent in the range and degree of his participation in the activities and forms of knowledge that men share.  ❧

# 8

## CONFESSIONS OF
## AN INQUIRING SPIRIT
## AND AIDS TO REFLECTION:

### Testament and Testimony

With the exception of a few excursions into the early career, this study has been concerned primarily with the period 1815–18, in which Coleridge wrote or revised most of the works, and made most of the publication decisions, that give his canon its familiar shape. Along the way, I have also suggested that the main themes and concerns of the later career—the relationship between reason and faith, between historical and prophetic Christianity, and between the Word and the Bible—all found definition during this period, subsuming into themselves the earlier psychological, poetic, and philosophical problematics which had proved, each in its own way, to be traps.

Of Coleridge's post-1818 publications, the best known and most influential is probably *Aids to Reflection* (1825)—an aphoristic work designed to guide the young man from simple notions of prudence, through concepts of morality, to an ultimate understanding and acceptance of Christianity. About the composition of *Aids*, Basil Willey tells us:

> The original intention had been to compile an anthology from Leighton's works, with brief notes and biography, to be called "The Beauties of Archbishop Leighton." As he proceeded, his mind and spirit caught fire; commentary

soon outgrew the texts, and Coleridge found himself writing a book on the process of reaching belief in Christianity. . . . *Aids* is in a sense a volume of marginalia on Leighton. By adopting the method of quotation and comment Coleridge shuffled off the constraints of formal treatise making, and attained, quasi-undesignedly, the freedom to be himself, and to do an important thing *tanquam aliud agendo*. Because he was supposed to be commenting on Leighton, he could produce, as if it were incidentally or as a side-issue, an introduction to Christianity far more effective than anything he could have done by direct attack.[1]

But *Aids* deserves to be seen as much more than a lucky accident, a more happy instance of Coleridge's shrinking into creation. For one thing, it frankly accepts, even boldly asserts, not so much the fact as the fitness of its debt to Leighton and of his continued presence. If we compare Coleridge's account of the composition of *Aids to Reflection* with his other myths of the origin of the text—the preface to "Kubla Khan" and *Biographia* XIII's "letter from a friend"—we are immediately struck by the lack of conflict between the work and the "history" with which Coleridge provides it. The potential for alienation, for dividing reading and writing, creation and awareness, inherent in analogies of poetry and prophecy, utterance and revelation, was the subject of "Kubla Khan."

The absence of such an antithesis between *Aids* and its history bespeaks Coleridge's abandonment of the analogies that set up a conflict between the historical and prophetic identities of his earlier texts. In *Aids to Reflection*, originality or creativity is analogous to commentary or interpretation. And Coleridge's confidence, amply supported in the text, in the capacity of interpretation to create beyond the limits of its object makes it unnecessary to repress the book's "natural parentage" or history since there need be no conflict between its worldliness and its value.

The interpretive stance is, finally, as "creative" as the prophetic stance because of the text's ability to support the simul-

1 Basil Willey, *Samuel Taylor Coleridge* (New York: Norton, 1973), p. 212.

taneous presences of Coleridge and Leighton, such that Coleridge's commentary on Leighton must also be treated as if it were no less the object of Leighton's commentary. Thus, this relationship suggests a view of literature as the concept sustaining the text's search for its completion in its proper interpreter or prophetic reader—the reader who defines and confirms its prophetic identity.

In all of this Coleridge is sustained by a view of the Bible that finds its most coherent expression in *Confessions of an Inquiring Spirit*—an epistolary essay published posthumously in 1840 by H. N. Coleridge. Originally, *Confessions* had been intended as a part of *Aids to Reflection* but was omitted because of its length.[2] Coleridge then included it among his projected *Six Disquisitions Supplementary to Aids to Reflection*.[3] Only one of these essays appeared in his lifetime, published in 1830 as *On the Constitution of Church and State*. *Confessions of an Inquiring Spirit* is especially valuable for us because it makes explicit in a sustained argument many of the points about Scripture which are implicit in or scattered throughout the text of *Aids to Reflection*. It is in the context of *Confessions* that we are able to see in the emergence of *Aids* out of an initial act of commentary the expression of an ideology and not just another accident of composition.

The argument of *Confessions*, heavily influenced by Eichhorn, is directed against the proposition that it is "necessary or expedient; to insist on the belief of the divine origin and authority of all, and every part of the Canonical Books as the condition, or first principle, of Christian faith" (*CIS*, p. 38). In response to this legalistic view, Coleridge asks:

> may not the due appreciation of the Scriptures collectively be more safely relied on as the result and consequence of the belief in Christ; the gradual increase—in respect of the particular passages—of our spiritual discernment of their truth and authority supplying a test and measure of our own growth and progress as individual believers, without

[2] Samuel Taylor Coleridge, *The Collected Letters of Samuel Taylor Coleridge*, ed. E. L. Griggs (Oxford: Oxford University Press, 1971), V, 435n.
[3] Letter, May 7, 1825; *ibid.*, 432–34.

the servile fear that prevents or overclouds the free honour      *177*
which cometh from love? (*CIS*, p. 38)


In order to test these propositions fairly, Coleridge says,
"I take up this work with the purpose to read it for the first time
as I would read any other work" (*CIS*, p. 41). In doing so, he
raises not only the question, What questions are proper both to
the Bible as the Word and to the Bible as the Book? He also asks,
What questions are proper both to the reading of the Bible and
to the reading of books in general? Thus, "Does reflection interfere
with faith?" and "Does the Bible's identity as a book interfere
with its identity as the Word?" are shown to be aspects of the
same issue: how are we to conceive the Bible as the paradigm for
textuality in all its manifestations?

Predictably enough, Coleridge argues that reflection makes
true faith (as opposed to blind, mean-spirited adherence) possible,
just as the Bible's identity as a book enables us to perceive it as
God's Word, despite apparent inconsistencies and contradictions.
Consider, Coleridge asks us, the Book of Job. Are we to see the
words of Job's accusers as equally the words of God—that is, as
equally true? If not, we must either give up the notion that all
Scripture is equally inspired; or we must conclude that some of
God's utterances are less true (or perhaps only less facetious) than
others. Such combinations of the Word and the narrative circumstance in which it is manifested are the basis for the perpetual
immanence in history of revelation and the faith based upon it.
In a sense, it is the presence of its contrary that gives the Word its
power to redeem, rather than condemn, our worldliness.

In this context, the New Dispensation proclaimed in the
New Testament, emphasizing the unity of the spirit over the
fragmentation of the letter, becomes the revision of Old Testament prophecy that gives the Bible its unity as a text rather than
as a collection of fragments. Combining questions of faith and interpretation, Coleridge turns the New Testament back upon the
Bible itself, revealing the internal act of reflection or revision that
makes possible our view of the Bible as an origin or Word and
gives it its textual identity.

If prophecy is subject to revision, then revelation does not precede the text—is not somehow closer to Godhead. Instead, it is through the textuality that sustains the Bible's dual identity as the Word and as a history of the Word that our conception of prophecy comes into being. In the gap defined by Coleridge between God's Word and the text actuated by his spirit, history arises and our culture begins. The origins of history in the doubleness of the text are, in part, the point of Coleridge's second initial proposition. There he offers the changes in our "spiritual discernment" of the truth and authority of certain passages as a "test and measure of our own growth and progress." On an analogy with the individual, whose identity is based on an awareness of his changing relation to the Bible—his history—Coleridge argues that the historical conception of human experience arises out of the antithetical identities of the Bible—an antithesis repeated in the relationship between language and textuality in all books.

Coleridge's concern with the role of the Bible in shaping the individual's conception of his own history, and especially his turning back of the New Dispensation on the Bible itself, reenter the realm of the historical (or to put it another way, the prophetic message is reassimilated to the historical identity of Christianity) by ranging themselves against the Protestant obsession (and certainly the obsession of Milton and Blake) with the Old Testament, conceived as a conflict between prophecy and history at the expense of the New Testament. In this way, *Aids* and *Confessions* become important statements for the next generation of Anglican clergy, even as they envision the terms upon which Coleridge's personal conflicts may be laid to rest.

For Coleridge, adherence to the letter is no guarantee of faith; rather, faith guarantees simultaneously the validity of the letter and our adherence. Confident in the quality of his belief, he is able to read the Bible as he would any other book without fearing for his faith. Beyond this and other assurances of his Christianity, Coleridge offers in *Confessions* even more profoundly personal testimony to the efficacy of his understanding of the Testaments. The opening paragraphs of *Confessions of an Inquiring Spirit*, still another myth of the origin of the text, include an extraordinary number of motifs from the earlier career—motifs his work that had plagued him throughout his career. Conceived of as a culmination or transcendence of mere humanity, poetry became for Coleridge a kind of confinement—a constant source of guilt. Recognizing this, he came to see that conceived as a species of prophecy, immutable and final, literature was in danger of coming to represent an ever-narrowing range of human possibilities—a constant prophecy of its own immanent and absolute irrelevance. In this context, the long struggle of Coleridge's career emerges as a rebellion against the most soul-destroying tendencies of his time.

# INDEX

Abrams, M. H., on the Greater Romantic Lyric, 34–35
*Aids to Reflection*, x, 83, 89, 174–76, 178

Bible, The, x–xi, 34, 47n, 83–84, 87, 89, 90–100, 106, 150–51, 152–55, 160, 161, 164–73, 174, 176–78
*Biographia Literaria*, viii, ix, 10, 17, 32, 83, 89, 100, 101–103, 121, 122, 134, 175, 180; original plan of, 1–3; imagination described, 4; imagination, primary and secondary, distinguished from fancy, 5–9; "letter from a friend," 11–14, 19, 23; on criticism and critical journals, 103–109; on the "two fundamental aphorisms of poetry," 112–16, 118, 136–37; volumes one and two compared, 135; on the "cardinal points of poetry," 136–41; origin of *Lyrical Ballads*, 141–43; definition of poem and poetry, 144–47, 151–52, 155; on imagination as reconciliation of opposites, 156–60; on Wordsworth's poetic diction, 161–65
Blake, William, 119–20
Bowles, William Lisle, 109–110, 111, 118, 122, 135

Brisman, Leslie, 25; on "letter from a friend," 11–12; on "Kubla Khan," 80–82, 86

"Christabel," viii, 1, 61–66, 74, 87
Coleridge, Samuel Taylor: and William Wordsworth, ix–x, 1, 2, 17–19, 59, 92, 102–104, 107, 108, 109–110, 114–15, 119–20, 122–29, 135, 140, 141–42, 147, 156, 161–65; and John Milton, ix, 46–47n, 59, 80, 83, 109–110, 118, 119–22, 128, 131–32
*Confessions of an Inquiring Spirit*, x, 84, 89, 176–81
Conversation Poems, The: defined and discussed in common, 34–37, 45; related to Mystery Poems, 59–60, 66–67, 73–74

"Dejection: An Ode," 45, 53–59, 180
de Man, Paul, on symbol, 21–22, 23–24, 87

"Eolian Harp, The," 37–41, 45, 58
"Essays on the Principles of Method," 15, 89, 146, 153–54, 165–69. See also *Friend, The*

*Friend, The*, 83, 151. See also "Essays on the Principles of Method"
"Frost at Midnight," 45, 52–53, 58

Hartley, David, 3–4
Hartman, Geoffrey, on Coleridge's "secondariness," 50n, 118–19
Hume, David, 98, 168–69

"Lines: On an Autumnal Evening," 129–34
*Lyrical Ballads*, Coleridge's account of their origins, 141–43, 147

Keats, John, "On Seeing the Elgin Marbles," 15
"Kubla Khan," vi, vii, viii, 1, 10, 13, 14, 61, 66, 116, 117, 157, 175, 180; preface to, 24–33; poem, 74–80; preface–poem relationship, 80–88

Milton, John (works): *Paradise Lost*, 10–11, 134; "Il Penseroso," 46; "On the Morning of Christ's Nativity," 120–21, 122; "Lycidas," 120, 125–26, 128, 131–32. *See also* Coleridge, Samuel Taylor
"Monody on the Death of Chatterton," 129
Mystery Poems, The, viii, 10, 34; distinguished from Conversation Poems, 36, 59–60; discussed in common, 37, 61, 66–67, 72, 87–88

"Nightingale, The," 45, 46–52, 58, 59, 74

Otway, Thomas, 57, 59

"Picture, The," 31, 85–86
Plato, "Allegory of the Cave," 19, 23, 180

"Religious Musings," 110, 118, 120–22, 135
Ricoeur, Paul: meaning distinguished from the conviction of meaning, 148; hermeneutics of faith and suspicion distinguished, 148n
"Rime of the Ancient Mariner, The," viii, 10, 13, 14, 19, 32–33, 61, 66, 67–74, 87

Schafer, Roy, on the word-surprise, 64–66
Schneidau, Herbert, on the Old Testament miracles, 101
Schneider, Elisabeth: on the literal truth of the preface to "Kubla Khan," 24; on "Kubla Khan" as a fragment, 24n
Shaffer, E. S.: on "Kubla Khan," 82, 86; on biblical orientalism, 171–72
*Sibylline Leaves*, 1–2, 9, 10, 16, 17, 40, 41
*Statesman's Manual, The*, 83, 89, 101, 106, 111, 115, 150, 154, 172; "tautegorical" defined, 7; symbol distinguished from allegory, 19–23; on the Bible, 90–100

"This Lime-Tree Bower My Prison," 41–44, 45
"To William Wordsworth," 122–29, 134

Watson, John, on the relationship between *Biographia* and *Sibylline Leaves*
Willey, Basil, on *Aids to Reflection* as a commentary on Leighton, 174–75
Wordsworth, William (works): *Prelude*, x, 1, 18, 102–103, 109, 115, 120, 122–29; Preface to *The Excursion*, 17–18; Preface to *Lyrical Ballads*, 107, 109, 115. *See also* Coleridge, Samuel Taylor

|           |                         |
|----------:|:------------------------|
| Designer: | Steve Renick            |
| Compositor: | Heritage Printers, Inc. |
| Printer: | Heritage Printers, Inc. |
| Binder: | Delmar Company          |
| Text: | Linotype Granjon        |
| Display: | Centaur/Granjon         |